Vermont Mountain Biking:
The best back road and trail rides in Southern Vermont

Dick Mansfield

Acorn Publishing
1063 Talmadge Hill South
Waverly, NY 14892

Cover Photograph by Brooks Dodge/MOUNTAIN STOCK

Special thanks to Cairn Cross of Guilford for assisting with the description of several rides and to Nancy Jean Steffen of Up & Downhill (Bennington) and George Plumb, Recreation Division Director, Vt. Dept. of Forest, Parks, and Recreation, for reviewing the manuscript.

Library of Congress Cataloging-in-Publication Data
Mansfield, dick, 1940-
    Vermont mountain biking : the best back road and trail rides in southern Vermont / Dick Mansfield
        p. cm.
    Bibliography: p
    Includes index.
    ISBN 0-937921-48-3 : $10.95
    1. Bicycle touring — Vermont — Guide-books. 2. All terrain bicycles. 3. Trails — Vermont —Guidebooks 4. Vermont — description and travel — Guide-books. I. Title
GV1045.5V5M36 1989   88-355596
917.43 — dc19   CIP

Contents

Southwestern Routes

West River Loops

Part 3   Resources

Introduction

Southern Vermont has hundreds of miles of dirt roads and trails that are lightly travelled and perfect for all-terrain bikes. The rides selected for this book were chosen as a result of my exploration and experience (having been born and raised in the area.) Included as well are the favorite spots of some of the region's avid cyclists. Routes were picked for ease of access and parking and for unique features such as swimming holes or lovely views. They are either loops or out and back tours, vary in length from under 10 miles to over 30, and are rated according to difficulty. Most of the rides are 100% dirt — only a few have brief sections on heavily traveled paved routes.

This book is designed for riders of all abilities. While I have ranked the rides as to ease, remember, this is Vermont. Every ride has some climbing and descending. Most rides have climbing early and in the middle, and then finish with a glide back to the starting point. Novices can take their time, push the bike up hills, and make a day of it. Hard charging experts looking for a workout can strap on an extra water bottle and blast off — there are some tough rides described herein.

Some routes are nested loops, that is, a shorter ride is contained within a longer loop. In such cases, information is repeated so that you don't have to flip back and forth.

As you ride these routes, you will encounter many inviting paths and trails that are on private land. Some of the best riding in Southern Vermont is on land owned by individuals, land which in many cases, might be open to responsible riders. Ask permission first, respect fences and gates, stay off the environmentally-sensitive terrain such as wetlands, muddy soils on slopes, and the Long Trail. NORBA, the National Off-Road Bicycle Association (now the U.S. Cycling Federation), developed this code for mountain bike riders:

1. I will yield the right of way to other non-motorized recreationists. I realize that people judge all cyclists by my actions.
2. I will slow down and use caution when approaching or overtaking another and will make my presence known well in advance.
3. I will maintain control of my speed at all times and will approach turns in anticipation of someone round the bend.
4. I will stay on designated trails to avoid trampling native vegetation and minimize potential erosion to trails by not using muddy trails or short-cutting switchbacks.
5. I will not disturb wildlife or livestock.
6. I will not litter. I will pack out what I pack in, and pack out more than my share whenever possible.
7. I will respect public and private property, including trail use signs, no trespassing signs, and I will leave gates as I have found them.
8. I will always be self-sufficient and my destination and travel speed will be determined by my ability, my equipment, the terrain, the present and potential weather conditions.
9. I will not travel solo when bikepacking in remote areas. I will leave word of my destination and when I plan to return.
10. I will observe the practice of minimum impact bicycling by "taking only pictures and memories and leaving only waffle prints."
11. I will always wear a helmet whenever I ride.

By using a little common sense and by respecting private land, mountain bike riders can help keep much of Southern Vermont open for off-road biking in the future.

As you use the book, perhaps you will want to suggest a favorite ride of your own. Send suggestions and corrections to Mountain Bike Guide, Box 7067, Syracuse, New York, 13261.

PART 1
Mountain Bike Basics

How To Buy A Mountain Bike

If you have a yen for a mountain bike, you'll find that when you go to buy, that you will have to shell out quite a few yen to get one. All-terrain bikes are very popular and comprise over half of the bicycles sold in many bike shops but they are far from easy on the pocketbook. You can easily get "sticker shock" when you first walk into a bike shop and take a look. It pays to do your homework before you open your wallet.

Retail prices for factory-made mountain bikes range from over $200 to over $1000. Because most frames and components are made in the Far East, the strong yen and weak dollar jumped the prices dramatically in the late 1980s and most popular models now sport higher price tags than their predecessors. Don't expect bargains on quality mountain bikes — as with any piece of quality recreational equipment, you tend to get what you pay for. Higher priced mountain bikes have lighter stronger frames and better components and are designed to take on any climb or descent that your legs and nerves can handle. They're the type I want under me on the back trails of the Green Mountain National Forest. Lower priced units are great for riding around town or traversing easy back roads.

Mark Perrin has assembled, repaired, sold, and ridden mountain bikes since they first hit the East Coast. He feels that for most people, buying an off-road bike is a lot like buying a canoe or a pair of skis. "The first thing I try to find out is just what the person plans to use the bike for. Some are shy about saying that they just want a bike for riding on the streets — with others it's pretty obvious that they'll be out in the mud and rocks with theirs. There are a lot of mountain bikes to choose from. It is a matter of matching a bike with their body, their planned usage, and their budget."

Pricing

Like most recreation gear, the best time to get a deal is before the season starts and after it ends. This is tough with mountain bikes since the season in the Northeast is long and bikes sell during the winter as well. The best bet, if you are determined to cut some costs, is to look for last year's models. Be careful with used bikes — many riders really abuse their mountain bikes and while a pre-owned bike may look fine, the poor thing is likely to be pretty tired.

For a mountain bike to be ridden mainly "around town," plan on spending $200 to $300. You'll get a straight-gauge steel frame and most components such as handlebars, control levers, and rims will be steel. You might want to buy smooth tires for it. The bike will probably weigh over 30 pounds — too heavy to tackle many of the steep hills in this book.

For tougher off-road riding on a lightweight frame, count on spending in the $500 range. The extra cost will get you a lighter frame and aluminum components. If mountain bike racing is in your future or you just want a light responsive bike to ride, plan to peel off 700 or more big ones. These bikes have sealed bearings, name components, and more "racy" frame geometry. At the high performance end of the spectrum, custom bikes start at over $1000 and go up from there.

Whatever you buy, a good bike shop will get you on a properly-sized bike, adjust it for you, and make any readjustments required after the initial break-in period.

Plan to spend at least $500 for a quality mountain bike

Bike Terms

When reading some of the cycling magazines listed in the
Resource section, it is easy to stumble over the "techno-talk"
often used to describe new models of mountain bikes. Writers
love to talk about head angles and seat post angles. (These
affect the bike's handling and responsiveness — too radical and
the bicycle is difficult to hand on the downhills, too conserva-
tive and it won't respond the way a skilled rider wants.) Another
favorite item for discussion is the chain-stay length. (Most
ATBs now have 17 to 17.5 inches — the shorter lengths
resulting in better climbing ability.)

But do you need to talk this language to be knowledgeable
enough to buy a mountain bike? Not really. If you deal with a

reputable shop, they will be up to speed on what's new and what's best for you. Listen up and don't hesitate to ask questions and shop around. Most designs have stabilized in the last few years and many of the models look similar. Try out different models with a test ride — you will find that some models just feel better to you. (It will probably be the highest priced ones that feel the best.)

There are several large mail order houses that sell mountain bikes. If you plan to deal with them, don't go around and pick the brains of bike shop technicians and then go out and phone in an order. Because of the wear and tear given mountain bikes and the need for periodic checks and repairs, it will, in the long run, pay you to buy from the shop where you'll be bringing the bike back to for adjustments and tuneups.

There's no big secret to buying a mountain bike — it is basically a common sense type of selection. There are several hundred models from which to choose, with more each season, but with a little exploration and test riding and by doing a little homework, you can find an 18 or 21-speed beauty that matches your physique and your pocketbook. Then it's all downhill (and uphill) from there.

Equipment

One of the joys of mountain bikes is that, like the old balloon-tire cruisers, they are easy to ride. You can just hop on and go without needing to fiddle with high pressure tires, to don Lycra shorts, or find your cleated shoes. Yet, in spite of this low-tech approach to riding, there are a few equipment items for you and your bike that will make touring the dirt roads and trails of Vermont safer and more enjoyable. Many are nice items for a gift list.

Helmet

Right at the top of the list, before you launch with a mountain bike, should be a helmet — leave your American Express card at home but not your helmet. A bike helmet is the most important piece of cycling gear you can own and thanks to today's technology, it can be light, comfortable, and stylish. While prices still hover in the $35 to $50 range for most, as one manufacturer's slogan goes: "If you have a $10 head, buy a $10 helmet."

Cyclists in the past complained that helmets were bulky, hot, and generally funny looking. That's all changed. Several years ago, GIRO Sport Designs produced the first Expanded Polystyrene-only helmet. EPS crushes on impact to take the shock and is also used in hard shell helmets. There are various designs, both in EPS-only and hard shell, so visit your bike shop and try several on. Make sure that your helmet meets the standards of the American National Standards Institute (ANSI) or the Snell Memorial Foundation. This is your sign of quality and assurance that the helmet will keep your cranium intact in most bicycle crashes.

Nearly all helmets can be customized to your head with padding and adjustable chin straps. Try several on and if possible, take one on a test ride. After a bit, you get so used to riding with one that you feel a little naked if riding without one. Notice, as you ride the trails and roads of Vermont — everyone with brains is wearing a helmet. It is just good old Vermont common sense.

Eye Protection

Aside from glare protection on sunny days, it is smart to

protect the eyes from foreign matter. Mountain bike tires can pick up and toss small pebbles and branches can whip across your face before you see them. There are many cycling sunglasses that work well and look racy while most bike shops also carry more inexpensive goggles. If you are riding off-road in rough terrain, give eye protection some serious attention.

Clothing

You can ride a mountain bike in any casual outdoor attire but always dress in layers. Vermont weather is changeable ("If you don't like this, wait a while and see what comes next.") This change is accentuated on a mountain bike for you not only have changes in elevation, but one moment you can be climbing with the sun on your back, sweating up a storm, and minutes later, be whipping down the other side of the hill in the shade with the wind sending shivers through you. A light windbreaker, stuffed in a fanny-pack or bike bag, can go a long way in providing comfort. A runner's trick is to stuff a large garbage bag in your gear just in case of sudden downpours — with a hole ripped for your head and two arm holes, it is an emergency poncho.

Gloves are used by most cyclists. While any light glove will do, cycling gloves are padded and comfortable and there are several inexpensive models available. In spring and fall, ski gloves are better suited because of the wind chill. Hands can get very cold on a mountain bike in inclement weather.

Cycling shorts have a padded crotch which, while essential for road bike riding, is not as important in mountain bike touring. Mountain bike seats are wider and more comfortable. Make sure that any shorts or pants are flexible and loose in the legs so as not to be restrictive. In colder weather, Lycra tights worn under shorts give extra protection.

Cycling shorts are designed for comfort and can double as walking shorts

Mountain bike shoes have reinforced uppers and stiff soles

Shoes

There are many mountain bike shoes available and while stiffer in the sole for support, they are also stiff on the wallet. All the rides in this book were ridden using good running shoes — that's all you need until you get into racing or expert riding. Avoid the "waffle-stomper" treads since they can be difficult to get in and out of when you use toe-clips.

Equipment Bag

As you know from visiting bike shops and reading catalogs, there are dozens of bike bags, from overnight panniers to small "fit-on-the frame" kits. Aside from a spare tube and repair gear, you'll want room to carry this book and such things as extra clothing. A fanny pack, the type worn by cross country skiers, can also be used for food, camera gear, and a windbreaker.

Frame Pump

While CO_2 cartridges and adapters are recommended in the maintenance section as being light and easy to carry, an air pump, designed to fit on the frame of your bike, is a nice equipment addition. It allows you to make small adjustments in tire pressure — for example to add air if you are going on a hard surface tour — and lets you save the cartridges for true emergencies. Make sure that the pump is designed for mountain bike tires and fits a Schrader valve.

Cycling Computer

Handlebar-mounted cycling computers are handy to help keep track of time and distance. You'll note that the rides in this book have many mileage checkpoints. That's when an odometer is handy — there aren't any mile markers on back roads and trails. Buy a simple one with a large easy-to-read digital readout. Make sure that the wires are taped to the fork (twigs and branches love to snag them) and make sure that you calibrate the computer to match the size of your wheel.

Bike Bottle

If you are riding much further than around the block, it's smart to carry water. A water bottle carried in a frame-mounted cage is not only inexpensive, it helps you replace fluids as you ride. Most mountain bikes come with braze-ons that allow you to easily bolt the cage to the frame. For longer tours, some riders mount two or more bottles on the bike, but you can also buy a larger bike bottle. Plan to carry several extra bottles in a cooler in the car so that you can re-hydrate after the ride.

Toe Clips

Experienced riders love toe clips. Clips allow more complete pedaling — you can pull as well as push with your foot. They also hold your foot on the pedal in muddy and wet conditions. New riders find them tricky since it's not always easy to get your foot out when you need to. Until you get comfortable on a mountain bike, you can feel "trapped" by toe clips. Plan to wear them loose at first, to allow easy dismounting, and avoid shoes with deep cleats that can get hung up in the pedal. It is a personal decision but the more you ride, the more you'll lean toward toe clips.

Tips on Riding

A pleasant mountain bike ride starts with a properly-fitted bicycle. Good bike shops will insure that your bike is not too large for you, that there is adequate clearance so that you will have room between your crotch and the top tube when you have to dismount in rough riding. Seat height is easy to adjust with the quick releases found on most seat posts and generally is a little lower than that for road bikes. As you pedal, your leg should have a slight bend in it at the lowest point in the pedal rotation. One way to check this is to sit on the bike beside a wall or a tree and back pedal, checking your leg extension. Another way is simple trial and error — adjust the seat, go for a little ride and see how it feels. Make sure that you tighten the seat quick release snugly or your seat may creep down slowly as you ride.

A good pair of tires can greatly enhance your mountain biking enjoyment, especially when you get on to rough roads or trails. Bikes usually come from the manufacturer with "plain vanilla" tires — whatever was in inventory at the time. These are fine for riding around town but may be too narrow for true off-road use. Talk to your bike shop — see what the experienced riders are using. (I like "Farmer John's" on the rear and "Ground Control" on the front.)

Tire pressure can affect your ride. Heavy riders need to carry a higher pressure than the lightweights. Too low a pressure can cause flats as the tire bottoms out against the rim and cause serious, expensive rim damage. The smoother the going, the higher the pressure should be. In muddy spring riding, when you need as much traction as possible, lower the pressure to 35 or 40 psi. Properly inflated fat tires with a good tread can make a world of a difference in bike handling.

Toe clips are a personal preference but the sooner you get a pair and get comfortable with then, the sooner you'll be able to handle the more difficult uphills and bouncy sections of a ride.

Technique

Mountain biking magazines run articles on the finer arts of bike handling in nearly every issue. While you may never feel the need to learn to do a "wheelie" or to bunny hop your bike up on a curb, you'll be thankful the first time you come upon a small log across a trail if you know how to get the front wheel up and over it. Check some of the periodicals listed in the Resource section and you will find some good riding advice. For most rides in this book, you'll be primarily concerned with getting better at climbing and descending — getting up a steep hill and then riding safely and enjoyably back down.

Let's look at climbing first. Body position plays a big role in climbing, especially if you are encountering loose gravel or slippery conditions. The theory is simple — just keep your weight distributed in such a way that the back wheel doesn't spin out and the front wheel doesn't lift off the ground. This means that unlike climbing on a road bike, where you can stand straight up on the pedals and rock the bike from side to side if needed, on a steep mountain bike climb you must crouch slightly and at the same time, keep your center-of-gravity aft. If you are too far forward, the weight goes off the back wheel and traction is lost. Conversely, if you sit back too far, you'll "pop a wheelie." It takes some experience since each hill is different.

Good riders stay on the seat while climbing

As you approach an uphill, anticipate by downshifting as you start into the hill so that you can keep pedaling with a good cadence. If you shift a little early or downshift too far, and the pedals spin, that's better than late. If you wait too long, you will have too much tension on the chain and may hear the derailleur make unkind noises as it tries to shift. (That's the voice of experience — I chewed up several freewheel teeth before smoothing things out.) There is a way to downshift if you goof and are grunting up the hill. It calls for a burst of power, by standing and accelerating, even for just a pedal turn. Then in one motion, sit down, back off the pedaling, and shift. By relaxing tension, you can downshift smoothly. Then get cranking at once in the lower gear.

Most good riders recommend staying on the seat as much as possible while climbing. When the trail gets too steep, stand up, with your body bent forward, and keep going. Because of the low gearing of mountain bikes, when you stand you usually can climb in a higher gear, and then shift as you sit down. The change from sitting to standing to sitting also saves the legs. Obviously, there are times when dismounting and pushing is the most effective — again it uses different muscles in the legs.

Descents are mountain biking's payoff for huffing up the hills. It takes some experience and confidence to enjoy them, especially when you look down and see washboard conditions or sharp curves. Again, like in climbing, body position is important. This is where you learn that a mountain biker comes in contact with three parts of the bike: the seat, the handlebars, and the pedals. The trick is to get the weight off the seat and the bars and onto the pedals. You want to ride in a crouch with your trunk slightly forward to keep your center-of-gravity back over the rear wheel to help with braking. Racers lower their seat and hang their rear out over the back wheel but for touring, it is just as effective to slide back so that you keep the rear of the saddle between your thighs. Ride with your pedals in the three and nine o'clock position and keep your weight on flexed legs, using your legs as shock absorbers, or else it will be hard to keep focused with your head bouncing. Your hands should be loose with a couple of fingers lightly on the brakes (so that you don't

Ride downhills in a slight crouch

inadvertently grab them from the bumps.) Use the rear brake first and handle the front brake, due to its sensitivity on downhills, gingerly. Riding downhill on a mountain bike can be a lot like skiing downhill, it is exhilarating once you get the hang of it.

So, get some good tires, get the bike adjusted to you, learn how to climb and descend, and you will be ready to handle any ride in this book, plus those of your own design, with confidence.

Mountain Bike Care & Feeding

"Ride it hard and put it away wet." That's the way many cyclists handle their mountain bikes. So often, after a long ride, we either let the dirt and mud dry on, to be knocked off later, or take the garden hose to the bike, and then roll the clean machine into the garage. That's no way to treat a horse, nor is it any way to treat a mountain bike. You may pay for it later on.

Mountain bikes are designed to run dirty and to take a certain amount of trashing. There is no need to fuss over them and keep them waxed and spotless. If you do, you may spend more time cleaning than riding. Yet, with a program of a few simple maintenance tricks, you can make sure that your bike will be ready to go again when you are. And it just takes a few minutes.

The key to maintaining mountain bikes is simple: keep the running parts cleaned and lubricated. Let's look at the cleaning tasks first.

Clean Machines

Most riders try to wash the grime off the bike after each off-road ride. If you use a hose, keep the pressure down and try not to hose down the sealed bearings or the freewheel. Give a little attention to the rims where the brake pads hit — if you keep them clean, you may save wearing out brake pads as fast, or scoring the rims from grit. Don't forget the bottom of the bike, especially where the cables go into the housing, and check the small wheels of the derailleur. When you are through with the water, dry the bike off with a rag. Then lubricate everything that moves. How much easier could that be?

Lubrication

The ubiquitous WD-40 is not the best lubricant to use since it tends to pick up a lot of dirt and is so thin that it washes off too easily when riding in wet conditions. Tri-Flow or a similar silicon or Teflon-based lubricant is better. Bike shops carry these and so might your local hardware store. After cleaning and drying the bike off, spray the drive train, the chain, derailleurs and all working parts. Buying Tri-flow is a lot cheaper than springing for new components.

There are several inexpensive chain cleaners that fit over a spray can of lubricant or, if you're frugal, you can use an old toothbrush. Run the chain through brushes to clean and lubricate it and wipe off the excess lubricant when you are through.

Bike shop technicians point out two special items that need attention every month or so. One is the seat post. Take the seat off and clean the post. Clean out the seat tube before reinstalling the post. One shop uses a gun cleaning rod and a rag, running it right down into the tube to clean out the dirt and moisture that accumulates there. Cover the seat post with a light coating of grease before reassembly.

Another potential trouble spot is the handlebar stem. To remove the stem, use a wrench to raise the bolt about a half inch and then tap the bolt to loosen the wedge. You should, if you have been doing preventive maintenance, be able to pull the stem out. Clean it and grease it. By doing this monthly, you can keep it from corroding and fusing in place.

Quick Checks

Mountain bike tires, with their lower pressures, don't leak air the way road bike tires do but it is wise to check their inflation periodically. Most mountain bike tires call for 35-65 psi of air but different conditions call for different inflation. Some recommend testing tires against a curb, with the front brake locked and your weight on the handlebars, to make sure that the tire does not bottom against the rim. Since there are few curbs in the woods, you also need to develop a sense of the tire pressure by squeezing the tire with your hand.

Brake pads should be checked for wear and adjustment. It is surprising how fast they can wear in harsh conditions. Make sure that you know how to adjust them so that the clearance with the rims is minimal.

Ten minutes of light cleaning and lubrication can save lots of repair bills later on. Give your mechanical steed a little care and feeding and a rubdown after each ride and it will be sitting there, waiting to go, the next time that you are. That's just simple mountain bike horse sense.

On The Trail Bike Repairs

Fortunately, for those of us not too mechanically inclined, the new breed of mountain bikes is quite hardy. The bikes require only periodic cleaning and lubrication to keep them happy. You can ride them all summer and never have trouble. That's the good news.

Here's the bad news. Imagine staring at your expensive TIG-welded mountain bike lying there, dead in its tracks, stopped by a stuck chain, or flat tire, or jammed derailleur. The deer flies buzz in and out of your hair as you wipe sweat from your eyes with muddy hands. The nearest pay phone is miles away. It's "fix it or push it time!"

The first repair truth is that the bike, if it breaks, will probably do it far from the car and when conditions for repairs are the worst. While breakdowns on the trail are rare, they never seem to happen at convenient times. There you are, deep in the glade. Why couldn't it happen when you just started out, or when you passed the farmhouse with the kid out front working on his BMX bike? Where is he when you need him?

The second truth is — if you have repair gear with you and know how to handle problems, the bike will run like a charm. But the day you get out the door without the spare tube, ... well, you've got the picture. Let's look at a few "on-the-trail" problems that you should learn to handle.

Chain Suck

Great term, isn't it? Somehow, the expression doesn't seem so coarse when it happens to you, when your greasy chain jumps off the front sprocket and gets stuck down between the crank and the frame. In fact, stronger terms usually are uttered. The key here is to take it easy and don't force the chain. First, take off your bike gloves to protect them. Get some slack from the rear derailleur and try to work the chain loose. With a little TLC and perhaps with the gentle help of a screwdriver or stick, you can usually get things back in shape in a couple of minutes.

Sticks and Mud in Brakes

If you are riding in mucky conditions, the tires can get pretty clogged with clay and mud which tends to collect on your brake arms. This is especially true if you have a low U-brake arrangement on the rear.

Don't worry about a buildup until it starts affecting the performance of the bike. If your wheels are dragging and are making a lot of whirring sounds from collected debris, just stop every so often and clean them out. Use a small stick or your fingers. Mountain bike brakes work surprisingly well, even

In adverse weather, periodically remove snow and mud from your brakes

when coated with wet mud. Just make sure to test them a few times before downhills to dry out the rims and pads before you need them.

Rear Derailleur

Rear derailleurs can get a little out of adjustment on a long hard ride, especially if you hit rocks and logs. Quite often, it is just a minor thing that sounds worse than it is and can wait until you are home or back at the bike shop. Other times, you may need to fiddle with the adjustments. (Many new systems have a simple process for minor adjustments, just turning a knob on the cable.) Derailleur adjustment is best learned directly from an experienced mechanic. Have a friend or your bike shop show you how it is done.

The most serious problem most mountain bikers face is derailleur failure. This can happen if you trash the derailleur on a rock or try to drag a maple limb through it. The chances are slim but if it does happen and you don't know what to do, you've got a long push ahead of you. First, you need a $3.00 chain tool in your kit. Use the tool to break the chain and then redirect the chain from the middle ring in the front to a middle gear on the freewheel. Take out some links to take up the slack and reconnect the chain. Take off the banged-up derailleur if you can and you're on your way in a single, middle-range gear.

Flat Tire

Mountain bike tires, in spite of their toughness, do get flats. Fixing them is easy, especially if you save the "patch-the-tube" fix until you get the bike home and instead, use a replacement tube for a quick on-the-trail fix.

First, unhook the brake cable so that the wheel can be removed and loosen the axle nuts or the quick release lever to remove the wheel from the drops. Use a tire lever to pry the sidewall away from the rim, breaking the connection, and continue to use the lever, or several of them, to free one side of the tire. (You should practice this at home before venturing too far — try to have someone demonstrate it once and you'll get it easily.) Remove the damaged tube and check the tire to make sure that there is no nail or glass imbedded which will ruin your new tube. Line up the valve of the replacement tube with the hole in the rim, carefully stuff the tube in the tire, and reseat the tire on the rim by rolling it up with your fingers. You may need a tire lever to finish the job. Reinflate the tire using a frame pump or a CO_2 cartridge and you are ready to put the wheel back on. Remember to connect the brake cable again and you are on your way.

Carry enough equipment to handle basic repairs

What To Carry

Most mountain bike riders carry a small pack that fits either on the frame or behind the seat. Here is a minimum list of equipment for off-road riding:

Small rag/ tissues/Band-Aids
Water bottle —filled
Bug dope
Spare tube
Frame pump
CO_2 cartridges
Tire levers
Chain tool
Adjustable wrench
Allen wrench Set
Small screw driver
Dog Repellant (optional)

The key to emergency bike repair is — **Be Prepared**. What works for the Boy Scouts also works well for mountain bike riders. A smattering of repair knowledge and a little preparation before the ride can keep your bike up and running.

PART 2

Mountain Bike Rides

Degree of Difficulty

Class 1   Mostly flat

Class 2   Moderately hilly

Class 3   Hilly with challenging climbs and descents. Some climbs may require walking. Suited for riders who are fit.

Class 4   Steep hills and technically demanding sections. For the accomplished mountain biker.

Southeast Loops

Ames Hill (*10 Miles Class 2*)
Carpenter Hill (*9 Miles   Class 3*)
Green River (*14 Miles Class 3*)
Halifax (*30 Miles Class 3*)
Marlboro Loops
        Marlboro 1 (*10 Miles Class 3*)
        Marlboro 2 (*14 Miles Class 3*)
        Marlboro/Dover (*13 Miles Class 2*)
Putney Mountain Ride (*10 Miles Class 3*)
Putney River Road (*11.5 Miles Class 1*)

Ames Hill Loop (10 miles   Class 2)

Short Summary
A short hilly tour past dairy farms and orchards of rural Brattleboro. Several long climbs on dirt roads.

Directions To Start
From I-91 Exit 2 in Brattleboro, head west on Route 9 to West Brattleboro. Park next to the Fire Station in the large lot.

Full Description
Pedal west on Route 9 for .2 miles and turn left on Greenleaf Street, across from the bank building. The initial climb will be on pavement with little shoulder so watch for traffic. Then you will have a half mile of rolling terrain before arriving at the intersection with the Abbott Road at mile 1. Take the dirt road straight ahead and start climbing up past an old farmhouse.

The farmland you are passing was preserved from development into a golf course and condominiums by the efforts of local residents and the Vermont Land Trust. After a half mile of climbing, the road levels and you soon will have some nice pastoral views of one of the few remaining dairy farms in Brattleboro. At mile 2.2, after a nice short descent, you will meet the Ames Hill Road.

The next mile is shady and gradually rising with one short climb up to a working dairy farm. Here is where the climbing starts. You have two steep hills ahead, broken by a stretch of easier climbing, ending at the apple orchard where you will turn left at mile 4. Pedalling along the flat stretch by the orchard, you will have lovely views of the farm ponds and, if it is clear, the mountains of New Hampshire. After passing another small farm at mile 4.5, you will see a long climb ahead. You will be turning left about half way up the hill.

You will pass several working dairy farms on Ames Hill

Turn to the east at the unmarked road that has a trailer just above it. — it appears to be a private road but it is a Class 4 road and a public right-of-way. Pedal down a quarter mile and you may come to a chain across the road near a new home. Ride by it and continue straight ahead on the trail. You now have a short downhill on a jeep trail before coming out of the woods near a large white house and an improved dirt road. This is the start of a great downhill run. Pass by the turn to the 4H camp and enjoy some steep descents followed by gentle sections until you intersect Hinesburg Road at mile 6.2.

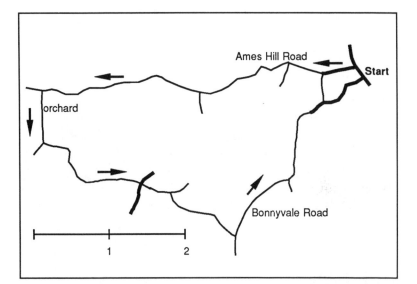

Carefully cross the main road and descend on Akley Road, turning right at the first intersection. You will have some easy back road riding for nearly a mile. As you approach your next turn at the Bonnyvale Road, there will be a pretty meadow lined with maples on your right.

Turn left on Bonnyvale and you will be facing a steep climb of a half mile. It gets a little easier as you near the top and at the crest, pause to catch your breath and note how the road was cut right out of the ledge — there will be outcroppings on both sides.

The trip back to West Brattleboro starts down steeply. After a long downhill, you will climb and come to an intersection at mile 8.4. Take a left and continue down past an orchard, cruising back to town as the road becomes paved. You will intersect Route 9 just west of your car so turn right and pedal to the start. There is a store and restaurant just across the street if you worked up an appetite on this short but challenging ride.

Carpenter Hill Loop (9 Miles Class 3)

Short Summary

Suited for a morning or summer evening ride when you only have a few hours to spare, this ride passes the Green River swimming hole about half way so bring your swim suits along. Be prepared for a couple of steep climbs and descents. Look for good local valley views. This ride shares part of its beginning and end with the Halifax loop and the Green River loop. If you would like a slightly longer ride with more climbing and descending, try the Halifax loop.

Directions To Start

From Exit 1 off I-91 in Brattleboro, go south on Route 5 for 2 miles to the hamlet of Algiers. (Algiers, nicknamed for the former pirate hangout in northern Africa, was once noted for the notorious card games that took place in the building at the intersection.) Turn off Route 5 onto the Guilford Center Road and proceed on pavement for another 4 miles. Your starting point is at the Guilford Elementary School and Town Offices which are located off to the right as you approach Guilford Center. Look for a right turn with a sign — the school/office complex is less than half a mile up the road.

Full Description

From the Guilford Elementary School, head back downhill on pavement. At .4 miles, turn right onto the paved Guilford Center Road. As you climb the slight upgrade, you will see the

Broad Brook Grange on your right and the Guilford Historical Society on your left. You'll be returning to this spot at the end of the loop. (Guilford was a Tory hot-bed during the Revolution. You might want to stop either before or after the ride and talk with a volunteer about it. Call the Town Clerk at 802-254-6857 or check the sign out front for business hours.)

As you continue the shallow climb on pavement past the Historical Society building, the pavement ends at 1.2 miles and the road forks. Take the right fork and get ready for some short steep climbs. Watch for farm dogs as you start up — we've encountered a few barkers who were guarding their turf. This is the Green River Road which winds uphill in a series of short steep climbs past dairy and sheep farms and country residences. Be sure to ride your lowest gears, the "granny gears," and now and then stop and look back at the valley you're leaving behind. At 2.3 miles, there's a small sheep farm on your right that is interesting to note because of the farming practices of the proprietor. After shearing time and during cold weather, this farmer dresses his sheep in fiberfill jackets to protect them from the cold. Keep on the lookout for these well-dressed sheep.

At 2.6 miles, after a final short but tough climb, you'll crest the hill and come to the Green River Forge. This working forge produces door hinges, implements, and sculptures by hand using time-honored traditions. As you pass the forge, get ready for a steep descent into the Green River Valley. It's brake check time, folks! Stay loose on the handlebars and brake levers and keep your weight back, watching for washboard conditions and potholes. This is a nice long downhill, ending rather abruptly at mile 3.7 as you enter the picturesque hamlet of Green River. The left fork drops down to a covered bridge while the right, the direction of the ride, passes the Green River Church. Green River is a fine spot for a picnic and a swim. If you are interested

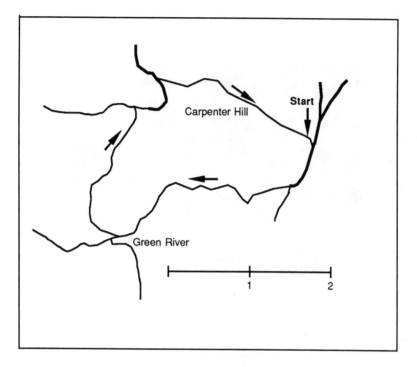

in getting wet, cross the covered bridge (noting the mailboxes inside the bridge.) There is good swimming in the small pond just upriver from the dam although many prefer the pools downstream.

When you want to press on, take the right fork of the Y and head north past the church. (If you did stop to wade, cross the bridge once more and turn left, north.) The dirt road parallels the Green River from time to time along this stretch and with the shade formed by the trees, it's a pleasant ride on warm days. At 5.7 miles, you'll come to a fork in the road. Make a right turn onto the Hinesburg road

Less than a quarter-mile from the intersection, just before the road becomes paved, you will pass a big farmhouse on the left.

Green River is a fine spot for a picnic and swim

This was the boyhood home of U.S. Olympic skier and silver medalist Bill Koch. Take advantage of this hard surface because it won't last long. This is a lovely section of southern Vermont with the meadows of the Hinesburg Brook off to your left. The big brown farmhouse you pass was once way up the hill and eighty years ago, was carefully winched down to its present location.

Right after the farmhouse, at 6.2 miles, look for the right turn on to a steep dirt road. This is Carpenter Hill Road (unmarked) and it is a steep half mile climb. Gear down and break up the climb with some rest stops to enjoy the view unfolding on your right. At 6.6 miles there is a cart path off to your right which leads to one of the many old Guilford cemeteries. Whether you are a gravestone buff or not, it's a peaceful place to visit and provides a welcome break and wonderful view of the Green

River Valley. At 6.7 miles, the hill crests and you begin a steep woodsy shady downhill. Again, it is brake check time and time to watch out for washboard and rutty sections.

This is a nice long descent in stages, broken by flatter sections, back to the Guilford Center Road. At 8.2 miles, you will come upon a small bridge. Slow down and use caution for it has a wooden planked surface separated to accommodate automobile tires. Just beyond the bridge on the left is an old brick schoolhouse, one of the many that used to be in service in Guilford. As you reach the end of the Carpenter Hill Road the scene should look familiar. The Historical Society building is across the paved road and the Broad Brook Grange is down the road to your left. Make a left turn and proceed down the hill on pavement for several hundred yards, turning left at the sign for the Guilford town offices. Pedal up the last .4 miles to the school where you left your vehicle.

Green River Loop (14 Miles   Class 3)

Short Summary

Nested within the longer Halifax loop, this ride goes in the opposite direction. This is a hill climber's special, in fact, it might be nicknamed "Short Cut Over The Mountain." You'll find out why when you ride it. The loop starts with 3 miles of level riding, has a series of fairly steep climbs in the middle, and ends with a long lovely descent into the hamlet of Green River which has a swimming hole and picturesque covered bridge.

Directions To Start

Green River is a small hamlet located 9 miles south of West Brattleboro. From Exit 2 of I-91, head west on Route 9 for 1.2 miles turning left on to Greenleaf Street. Stay on the paved road, the Hinesburg Road, until you pass West Guilford. Keep going until the road turns to dirt and then take the next left and drive the two miles to Green River. Parking is restricted within 100 yards of the covered bridge so drive across it, turn left, and you will find ample parking along the road that parallels the river.

Full Description

The ride starts right at the covered bridge and heads across it toward the church, then turns north up the rolling dirt road that you just drove down. Follow the Green River upstream for 2 miles until encountering a fork in the road. Go left, keeping the Green River off to your left.

This stretch of road is flat and shady. (You will ride it in the opposite direction if you try the Marlboro 2 loop.) As you pedal along, you can see some very inviting places to wade. At mile 3, you will come to a small bridge on your left that crosses Green River. This is Wrights Road (unsigned). Why not stop and admire the water for a moment? There's a big climb ahead.

Did I lie? This is a steep quarter-mile climb with some soft sections so gear down and keep your rear wheel weighted. Ignore the left turn at the top of the rise and just keep chugging straight ahead. The climb continues for a mile. Now you can see why the nickname, "Short Cut Over The Mountain," fits.

After an all-too-brief downhill, you'll pass a road that continues off to the right. Bear left, staying on the main road which is now the unmarked Deer Park Road, and keep up the climb. At mile 5.0, you'll approach a farm/summer home complex that comprises the "place" of Deer Park. Have faith, the top of the climb is just ahead. Now you get a short downhill to recover. Deer Park Pond will be off to your right as you pedal down. The pond is strewn with lily pads and duckweed and hundreds of frogs sunning themselves on a good day. Just after the pond, there's a small cemetery on the left with about 20 gravestones. It is interesting to note that the name "Wilkes" is spelled four different ways. Look for a quiet little pond at mile 5.9 on the left, ringed by dead spruces. It is picture-book Vermont, thanks to some energetic beavers.

After one more climb past a farmhouse (watch out for the dog — it is noisy but friendly), you have a long descent of a mile, with one left turn during the downhill, into the hamlet of Halifax. At the four corners in Halifax, take a moment to look at the small white church called the Halifax Union Society, erected in 1853. The woodwork inside is lovely.

Turn left (east) by the row of mailboxes that mark Stage Road. You'll immediately pass the a cemetery and climb out

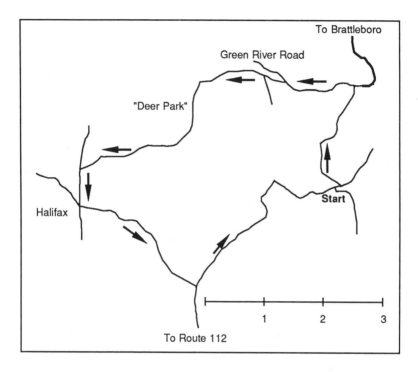

of Halifax past some handsome summer and year-round homes. After several downhills and some nice views, you will come to an intersection with a sign pointing to the right for "Route 112" and to the left for "Green River."

You have gained a lot of altitude in this ride so far — after a half mile of level riding, you'll start down. About a mile later, at mile 12, you will pass the Hollandia Farm on your left and begin another great downhill ride. Caution, there are several steep sections with turns. The road crosses a small brook at mile 13.1 and after a short stretch of level riding, you will descend down the flank of Pulpit Mountain directly into the Green River hamlet. What a spectacular ending to a mountain bike ride. Why not park the bikes and take a swim by the dam?

Halifax Loop (30 Miles   Class 3)

Short Summary

This loop is suited for a full day's tour. Bring your lunch and plenty of water because there are no facilities along this loop even though you'll pass through several very small villages. Bring your swimming suit and take advantage of some streams and rivers along the way. This ride shares part of its beginning and end with the Carpenter Hill loop and traverses parts of the Green River and Marlboro routes.

Directions To Start

From Exit 1 off I-91 in Brattleboro, go south on Route 5 for 2 miles to the hamlet of Algiers. (Algiers, nicknamed for the former pirate hangout in northern Africa, was once noted for the notorious card games that took place in the building at the intersection.) Turn off Route 5 onto the Guilford Center Road and proceed on pavement for another 4 miles. Your starting point is at the Guilford Elementary School and Town Offices which are located off to the right as you approach Guilford Center. Look for a sharp right turn — the school/office complex is less than half a mile up the road.

Full Description

From the Guilford Elementary School, head back downhill on pavement. At .4 miles, turn right on to the paved Guilford Center Road. As you climb the slight upgrade, you will see the Broad Brook Grange on your right and the Guilford Historical

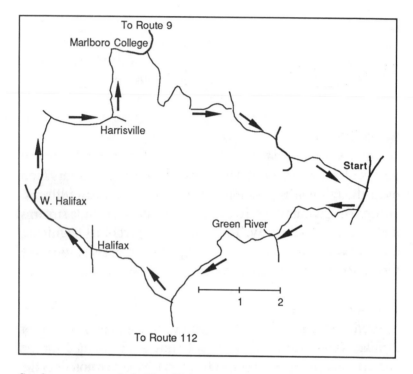

Society on your left. You'll be returning to this spot at the end of the loop. (Guilford was a Tory hot-bed during the Revolution. You might want to stop either before or after the ride and talk with a volunteer about it. Call the Town Clerk at 802-254-6857 or check the sign out front of the building for business hours.)

As you continue the shallow climb on pavement past the Historical Society building, the pavement ends at 1.2 miles and the road forks. Take the right fork and get ready for some short difficult climbs. Watch for farm dogs as you start up — we've encountered a few barkers who were guarding their turf. This is the Green River Road which winds uphill in a series of short steep climbs past dairy and sheep farms and country residences.

Be sure to ride your lowest gears, the "granny gears," and now and then stop and look back at the valley you're leaving behind. At 2.3 miles, there's a small sheep farm on your right that is interesting to note because of the farming practices of the proprietor. After shearing time and during cold weather, this farmer dresses his sheep in fiberfill jackets to protect them from the cold. Keep on the lookout for these well-dressed sheep.

At 2.6 miles, after a final short but tough climb, you'll crest the hill and come to the Green River Forge. This working forge produces door hinges, implements, and sculptures by hand using time-honored traditions. As you pass the forge, get ready for a steep descent into the Green River Valley. It's brake check time, folks! Stay loose on the handlebars and brake levers and keep your weight back, watching for washboard conditions and potholes. This is a nice long downhill, ending rather abruptly at mile 3.7 as you enter the picturesque hamlet of Green River. The left fork drops down to a covered bridge, the direction of the ride. Green River is a fine spot for a picnic and a swim. If you are interested in getting wet, cross the covered bridge (noting the mailboxes inside the bridge.) There is good swimming in the small pond just upriver from the dam although many prefer the pools downstream.

From the Green River covered bridge, head straight up the steep hill. (This downhill is the ending of the Green River loop.) You will pass the Pulpit Mountain Farm right away for you are climbing up the flank of Pulpit Mountain. After a climb of less than half a mile, the road levels off temporarily and there is a nice view off to the right. At 4.7 miles, the route crosses a small brook and you will begin a demanding climb of a mile with some steep sections. At mile 5.8, the Hollandia Farm is on your right and you can coast down the short downhill. Catch your breath during this brief respite for there is more climbing right ahead. Continue uphill until 6.9 miles where the road finally flattens out. Ride for a half mile until you come to a junction in the road.

Let's check our bearings. The road that you have been riding continues straight ahead and another road (unmarked) goes off to the right. There's a road sign which notes that Green River is behind you while Route 112 is ahead. Take the 90 degree right turn and climb steadily uphill. At 7.9 miles the road flattens again and at 8.1 miles there is a nice view off to the left. Your can see south and west into Colrain, Massachusetts. The Hoosac Range of the Berkshire Mountains is visible on the far horizon on a clear day.

You now will come to some rolling terrain — short climbs interspersed with short downhills — great mountain bike riding. At 9.3 miles, start a steady descent into the community of Halifax. You'll pass several lovely country homes on your descent and just before you get to the hamlet, pass an old cemetery on the right. Is it time for a little gravestone reading or a lunch break?

At 9.8 miles, you will come to the four way intersection in the town of Halifax. Note the local news bulletin board on your right detailing what's going on in this small rural community. You may want to take a moment to look at the small white church off to the left called the Halifax Union Society, erected in 1853. The woodwork inside is lovely.

To resume, proceed straight through the intersection (actually the road jogs a bit to the right) and continue downhill on gravel until 10.5 miles. At this point, it's flat riding for a quarter of a mile and then, after a short climb, you will have a gradual descent to pavement. Get ready for a steep fast downhill on pavement into West Halifax. After a half mile of downhill, your road will be joined by a main road through West Halifax. After pedaling past the white elementary school on the left and in short order, the West Halifax Bible Church and the fire station, take the next right turn, still on pavement, and follow this rolling twisting paved road, enjoying the reduced friction of pavement for the next two miles.

At 13.8 miles, you'll again encounter dirt and a quarter mile later, come to a "T." The sign shows Jacksonville off to the left, and Brattleboro to the right. Take the right and descend past a farm on your left and get ready for a gradual climb. At 15.4 miles, you'll come to the hamlet of Harrisville, reaching a sign that says Marlboro College next to a road leading to your left. Make the left turn and head toward Marlboro College. (This is part of the Marlboro 2 loop, in reverse.) You have some elevation to gain so enjoy some flat riding before starting the steep ascents up Ash Hill to Marlboro College. Famous for its summer concert series and musicians like Serkin, Casals, and Moyse, the college's whimsical sign, "Caution, musicians at play," greets you as you pass the campus.

Continue on the paved road past the college and pedal to where the paved road makes a sharp bend to the left. A dirt road bears off to the right — this is Lucier Road, part of the Marlboro 1 route. You've got a steady 1/2 mile climb on dirt up Chase Hill and then the road levels off a bit as you pedal through a section of hemlocks.

After a 1/2 mile downhill, you'll round a bend in the road and think you've arrived in someone's doorway. The road goes right by the end of a white summer home — this is the 19.6 mile mark. Stop for a moment and look off to the right (south) and see if you can find the old right-of-way down over the bank that used to be an active road. Old-timers chuckle when they describe going down it with a team of horses or later, with a Model T. It pitches down to the Green River Road. There are some weather-beaten farm buildings at this stopping point that you might note.

Start a climb to the northeast passing a modern home on your left. At the intersection at the top of the rise, turn right and pass the "Hoggett Hill Farm." You've just climbed Hoggett Hill. After a short level stretch, get set for a great downhill. Check

One of the weathered barns on Lucier Road

your brakes before you start down.

After the first descent, stop if you want and catch the view off to the south, then start another very steep drop down Thomas Hill Road. Watch out for rutty sections as well as some softer sand areas as you descend. You'll shoot past several beautiful homes and just as you near the bottom, by an old cemetery. At the intersection, take a right turn and enjoy some great pedaling down the Hinesburg brook crossing a number of narrow bridges. At 23.6 miles you come upon the paved Hinesburg Road (unmarked.) Bear right down the pavement past the West Guilford Baptist Church and cemetery. Start watching for a dirt road off to the left. You will reach it at mile 24.

This is Carpenter Hill Road (unmarked) and it is a steep half mile climb. Gear down and break up the climb with some rest stops to enjoy the view unfolding on your right. Take heart, this is the last climb on this long ride. At 24.4 miles there is a cart path off to your right which leads to one of the many old Guilford cemeteries. Whether you are a gravestone buff or not, it's a peaceful place to visit and provides a welcome break and wonderful view of the Green River Valley. At 24.5 miles, the hill crests and you begin a steep woodsy shady downhill. Again, it is brake check time and time to watch out for washboard and rutty sections.

This is a nice long descent in stages, broken by flatter sections, back to the Guilford Center Road. At 25.8 miles, you will come upon a small bridge. Slow down and use caution for it has a wooden planked surface separated to accommodate automobile tires. Just beyond the bridge on the left is an old brick schoolhouse, one of the many that used to be in service in Guilford. As you reach the end of the Carpenter Hill Road the scene should look familiar. The Historical Society building is across the paved road and the Broad Brook Grange is down the road to your left. Make a left turn and proceed down the hill on pavement for several hundred yards, turning left at the sign for the Guilford town offices. Pedal up to the school where you left your vehicle. Motorized transportation probably never looked so good.

MARLBORO LOOPS

The hamlet of Marlboro, located ten miles west of Brattleboro, is an excellent starting point for back roads exploring. These three loops provide a good taste of southern Vermont dirt road riding. You'll see Marlboro College professors' homes, summer homes that have been in the same family for generations, and a number of old farms.

Marlboro 1 (9 Miles Class 3)

Short Summary
A short loop which features several long climbs and one steep downhill. Nice views from several locations.

Directions To Start
From I-91 Exit 2 in Brattleboro, head west on Route 9 for 7 miles, watching for the turn for Marlboro. Driving in from Route 9, you will find parking near the Marlboro Post Office and the white-spired Marlboro Meeting House. The Whetstone Inn, an 18th century inn, is next door. (802-254-2500)

Full Description
Begin by travelling south on the paved road toward Marlboro College. Once you pass the volunteer fire company building you'll know you're on the right track. The ride starts with a nice gradual downhill on pavement. After 1.4 miles, go straight on

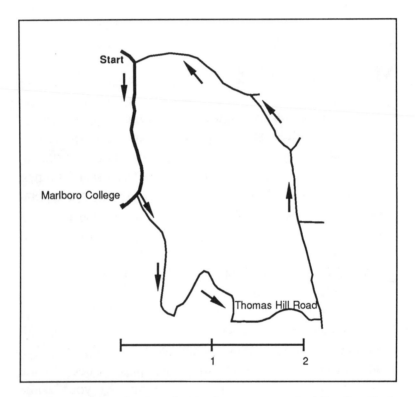

the dirt road (Lucier Road). You've got a steady 1/2 mile climb on dirt up Chase Hill and then a level stretch as you pedal through a stand of hemlocks.

After a half mile downhill, you'll round a bend in the road and think you've arrived in someone's doorway. The road goes right by the end of a white summer home just before the 3 mile mark. Stop for a moment and look off to the right (south) and see if you can find the old right-of-way down over the bank that used to be an active road. Note the weather-beaten farm buildings on your left at this stopping point.

Start a climb to the northeast at mile 3 passing a modern home on your left. At the intersection at the top of the rise, turn right and you will pass the "Hoggett Hill Farm." After a short level stretch to catch your breath, you're going to be treated to a breath-taking downhill.

After the first descent, stop if you want and catch the view off to the south, then start another steep drop down Thomas Hill Road. Watch out for rutty sections as well as some softer sand areas as you descend. You'll shoot past several beautiful homes and just as you near the bottom, by an old cemetery. At the bottom of the hill, you'll intersect Cowpath Road at mile 4.7.

There's no free lunch in mountain biking and yes, you're about to gain back some of that elevation that you just lost. You'll turn left at the bottom and start a steady climb back to Ames Hill. But before you do, you might want to stop and splash a little water from Hinesburg Brook on your face and fill your water bottle as you face the climb. The hills off to the east (right side as you climb) comprise Governor's Mountain, a Tory hideout during the Revolution where locals holed up with cattle to avoid conscription.

The climb starts with a mile of rolling uphills. Check out the old stone walls on each side of the road. At mile 5.8, you'll come to a white summer home with a road leading off to the right. As you continue the climb, you're approaching one of the prettier views in southern Vermont. When you top the final rise and coast down toward a cluster of homes at mile 6.6, pause by the small pond and look off to the left (west). Weather permitting, you'll see a great view of the Haystack/Mt. Snow area north of Wilmington. Take the left fork (the right is a private dead end) down a little hill and after a few rolling hills, you'll enjoy a straight downhill to Ames Hill.

At Ames Hill, turn left, west, and bike a mile and a half. Save something for the last climb — it is a real energy-drainer. Soon you'll see the steeple of the Marlboro Meeting House ahead.

Marlboro 2 (14 Miles   Class 3)

Short Summary

A hilly loop which passes by Marlboro College and then descends to the Green River valley before climbing back up to Ames Hill Road.

Directions To Start

From I-91 Exit 2 in Brattleboro, head west on Route 9 for seven miles, watching for the turn for Marlboro. Driving in from Route 9, you will find parking near the Marlboro Post Office and the white-spired Marlboro Meeting House. If you want to make an overnight of it, contact the Whetstone Inn for accommodations. (802-254-2500)

Full Description

As with the Marlboro 1 ride, pedal south from your parking spot on the paved road toward Marlboro College. Once you pass the volunteer fire company building you'll know you're on the right track. As you pass the Lucier Road turn for Marlboro 1, keep going on the pavement towards Marlboro College. Famous for its summer concert series and musicians like Serkin, Casals, and Moyse, the college's whimsical sign, "Caution, musicians at play," greets you as you approach the campus. Pedal on straight ahead past the school, taking the narrow dirt road that looks like a driveway (mile 2). The road will soon pitch down in a series of steep descents called Ash Hill. Expect some loose gravel and washboard conditions during the mile of downhill. The road then flattens and after a mile of easy pedaling, you will arrive at the hamlet of Harrisville at mile 4.

Turning left in Harrisville, follow the Green River Road for over 5 miles. This is easy riding along the stream and is generally downhill. Be alert for traffic for the road is well-traveled at times. There are a number of inviting spots along the way to stop and splash in the river if you are so inclined. At mile 7.4, you'll pass the Deer Park Road bridge on your right (Green River Loop) and a mile later, come to a little intersection with the road to the hamlet of Green River going off to the right. (It is a two mile pedal down to the covered bridge and dam if you want a side trip.) To continue on Marlboro 2, go straight ahead.

The hamlet of Green River is an easy side trip at mile 8.5

Shortly after you pass the intersection, just before the road becomes paved, you will pass a big farmhouse on the left. This was the boyhood home of U.S. Olympic skier and silver medalist Bill Koch. After a short stretch, you'll start on pavement for about a mile. This is a lovely section of southern Vermont with the meadows of the Hinesburg Brook off to your

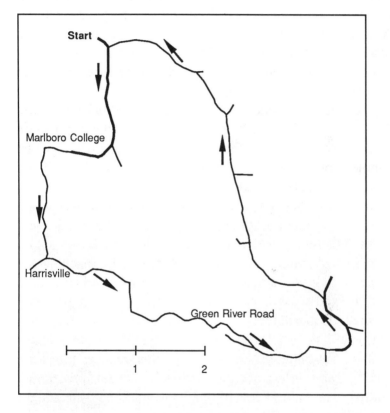

left. The big brown farmhouse you pass was once way up the hill and, eighty years ago, was carefully winched down to its present location. As you climb into West Guilford on pavement and pass the Baptist church, take the dirt road that goes straight ahead (mile 9.5). Note the house on the corner that was a blacksmith's shop for years. (The paved road that climbs out of West Guilford goes on toward Brattleboro as the Hinesburg Road.)

The dirt road you're on is called the Hales Brook Road by

some and it climbs gently for a mile and a half along the brook until you intersect the Marlboro 1 route at mile 11. It comes in on your left down Thomas Hill. (If you like steep hills, you can climb Thomas Hill and backtrack to Marlboro that way.) The hills off to the east (right side) comprise Governor's Mountain, a Tory hideout during the Revolution where locals holed up with cattle to avoid conscription and trouble.

After the intersection with Thomas Hill Road, the climb starts with a mile of rolling uphills. Check out the old stone walls on each side of the road. At mile 12, you'll come to a white summer home with a road leading off to the right. (That's Barrows road, also called Adams Road, a lovely ride down to Ames Hill but one that adds more miles and a two very tough climbs — perhaps next time.) Go straight ahead and at the next house, pull over, catch your breath, and look back behind you at the view. As you continue the climb, you're approaching one of the prettier views in southern Vermont. When you top the final rise and coast down toward a cluster of homes, pause by the small pond and look off to the left (west). Weather permitting, you'll see a great view of the Haystack/Mt. Snow area north of Wilmington. Sunsets from this vantage point are striking. Take the left fork (the right is a private dead end.) down a little hill and after a few rolling hills, you'll enjoy a straight downhill to Ames Hill. Let the bike run — you've earned it.

If, after that climb, you've got plenty of time and energy, you might consider a short diversion in to one of the prettiest bodies of water in the area, South Pond. Take a sharp left in through the stone pillars and follow the dirt road in about a mile. Bear left at the one intersection. The land around the pond is controlled by a private association but there is a public access fishing area where you can look and if you'd like, wade.

Back at Ames Hill, turn left, west, and bike a mile and a half.

The Marlboro Meeting House marks
the start and finish of Marlboro loops

The last climb is a real energy-drainer after a long ride so save
something in reserve for it. Soon after you crest the hill, you'll
see the steeple of the Marlboro Meeting House ahead and then,
after a short downhill and climb, you'll be back to the starting
point. You've had a good taste of southern Vermont hills and
back roads.

Marlboro/Dover Loop (13 miles   Class 2)

Short Summary

A relatively easy loop along quiet back roads that are steep in the middle section. The ride is easily accessible off Route 9 and offers some lovely views.

Directions To Start

From I-91 Exit 2 in Brattleboro, head west on Route 9 for 12.1 miles. Go past the turn for Marlboro and watch for the sign for the Southern Vt. Dairy Goat Assn. Just down the road, still on Route 9, there's a parking area on the left (3.3 miles from the Marlboro turnoff.) From Wilmington, go east past Hogback Mountain and look for the parking area on your right as you finish the long sweeping downhill.

Full Description

Carefully cross busy Route 9 and travel west for several hundred years to the dirt road (Cross Road) that goes off to the right past the small pond and white farmhouse. The first mile of riding is generally flat along some pretty meadows, passing several restored farmhouses. At mile 1, you'll ride over the tiny Bellows Brook and after an easy climb and descent, arrive at the intersection with Higley Hill Road (unmarked). Turn right and coast for a little less than a half mile down the hill. The next turn will be a sharp left just after the steep downhill. (Mile 1.8)

The wooded road will climb gently for the next 1.3 miles, passing a horse farm at mile 2.4 and then opening up into farm

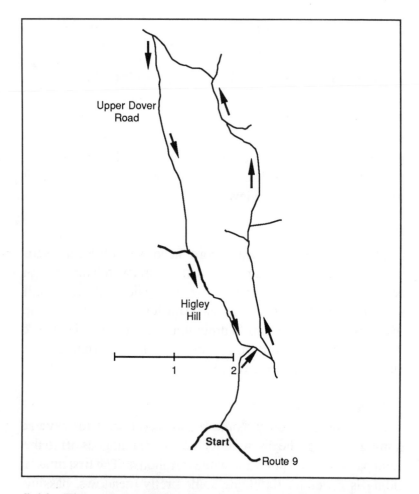

fields. There are a number of homes, new and old, along this section and at mile 3.2, you'll see a long beautiful downhill ahead. The route crosses Worden Brook and then intersects with a road from the right.

There's some climbing ahead through a wooded section with many mature pine trees scattered among the hardwoods. Stonewalls line the route as you climb for .6 miles. As the road levels on top, there are a couple of nice views off to the east. Stay on the main road as you pass the Hunter Brook Road and a brook at mile 5.1. As you pass a number of homes and camps in this section, you're approaching the hilliest section. There are two tough climbs and one steep downhill along the narrow road. Watch for washboard conditions and loose gravel.

As you labor up to a large old farmhouse on the left, take the left turn onto Captain Copeland road (unmarked). After a steeper climb to mile 6.8, you'll meet a dirt road that goes off to the left. That's the road back. It will be easier and have some nice views. But first you have to climb a little more.

This is the Upper Dover Road which narrows as you ride along. The first half mile features rolling terrain. Then there is some serious climbing but soon you will be rewarded with some wonderful views of the hills off toward New Hampshire including, if the weather is clear, a nice look at Mt. Monadnock. At mile 7.7, you'll level off and enjoy a mile of level riding past a number of homes, all with wonderful vistas off to the east. As you transition to some ups and downs approaching the Higley Hill road intersection (mile 8.9), the road is shaded and narrow. The climbs are over; soon you'll be getting some downhill riding. At mile 9.6, the paved Higley Hill road will come in from your right so bear left and watch for traffic. After some gentle rolling terrain with a good view off ahead and to the left, start down the long downhill for a good half mile. Be ready for the transition to dirt at mile 10.2 as the road continues down. Then you have some easy riding as you pass quite a few homes and at mile 11.1, an active beaver dam and pond.

At mile 11.3, take a right onto the road that you began the ride on. Climb up the rise, coast down, and enjoy some easy riding, retracing your route back to Route 9. If you've worked up an appetite, Skyline Restaurant is just up Route 9 to the west.

Putney Mountain Ride (10 Miles   Class 3)

Short Summary
A short ride suited for riders who are fit. A long climb, partially on pavement, followed by a section of technically-demanding trail riding with a long descent to the start.

Directions To Start
From Exit 4 off I-91, take Route 5 to the Village of Putney. At the center of Putney, take the left toward West Hill/Putney School and proceed .8 miles to the Putney Central School. Parking is available at the area north of the complex or if school is in session, at the swimming pool area south of the building.

Full Description
Turn right from the parking lot and head north on the paved road, taking the first left turn, West Hill, which climbs toward Putney School. This will be a steady climb with some fast moving traffic at times so be alert. The first mile takes you huffing past Green Mountain Orchard and shortly afterward, you start pedaling past the ski trails of Putney School. The school, long a hotbed of cross country skiing (Koch, Caldwell, etc.), is situated high to your left as you climb. Local riders use some of the ski trails for off-road biking but the trails are private and not available, without permission, to the public. Pass by the turn for the school and continue ahead on pavement.

At mile 2, you will come to the intersection of West Hill and Aiken Road so continue to the left and cruise down the shallow paved downhill, looking for the Putney Mountain Road turn at mile 2.6. Turn right on the dirt road and continue past the Holland Hill Road, which heads off to the left.

As you climb up the narrow road that parallels the brook, you will find that the climb gets steeper as you continue. You'll be climbing up through a hardwood forest and at mile 3.3, will come to an intersection. The trail that goes off to the left is a good one to try — it connects with the Holland Hill Road.

Pedal and push upward for another mile to the Banning Road which will be a right turn. This is an interesting area for stone walls. When you notice the patterns of the barnyards and pastures, it is easy to picture the hill farms, many of them with sheep, that were here before the forests took over again. (Groups of men would come to an area like this with their teams of horses and stone bolts and custom build stone walls for the farmers. They certainly were busy here.)

Notice the white birches at this elevation as you cruise. At mile 3.9, there are several summer homes on the right with lovely views off to the mountains of New Hampshire. A quarter of a mile later, the road swings to the right (the wider road to the left is a driveway) and becomes narrow. You will come to a new home as the trail begins with a rocky wet downhill section.

The next several miles is great mountain bike terrain and typical of the riding that you can find up on this ridge. After the first rough downhill, there's an intersection with a jeep trail heading down the hill to the right and another climbing gently to the left. Take the left fork and ride through some wet sections before climbing up to the plateau. As you level, you'll come to the remains of an old hunting camp. Pull off to the right into the small clearing and you will have a nice view to the east.

After a half mile more of trail riding with several bony down-hills, you will come to another intersection marked by stone

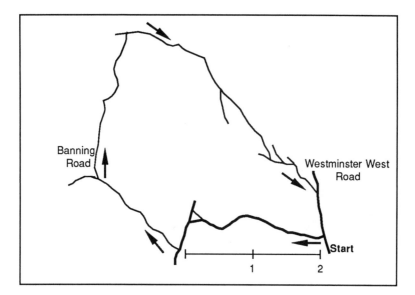

walls. Take the right down the hill towards Putney. There will now be a half mile of rutted jeep trail with several very rocky sections to navigate. It is interesting downhill riding all the way to mile 6 when you will intersect an improved road with a house to your right. Bear left down the hill.

In less than a quarter mile, take the right at the intersection and climb up by the Wyngate Farm before starting a long downhill. The next mile will be predominantly down with a couple of shallow climbs. At mile 7.2, take the left down Brook Road and enjoy another 1.3 miles of shallow descent along the brook. As you roll to another intersection, pedal straight ahead on the wider Tavern Hill Road, pass the Black Locust Road, and when you come to the next junction, turn right on the pavement.

You will climb up past the Hickory Ridge School and then glide down, intersecting with the Westminster West Road at mile 9.1. Turn right and it is a flat ride back to the school.

River Road Ride (11.5 Miles   Class 1)

Short Summary

A short loop which follows the Connecticut River and then has some gradual climbs and descents back to the start.

Directions To Start

From Exit 4 off I-91, head to the Village of Putney. Continue north on Route 5 for 2.5 miles. At the bottom of a long winding descent, you will come to the East Putney Brook Road. There is parking just off Route 5 on the right side.

Full Description

Pedal east on Route 5 across the brook and take the paved road, East Putney Falls Road, which heads off to the right. Cruise down along the brook, passing a number of houses and crossing under the interstate before you come out on the Connecticut River plain and intersecting with River Road at mile 1.6. Turn left and enjoy some easy riding on the smooth road. The Boston and Maine railroad tracks parallel your route on the right and further over is the river. Be alert for fast-moving traffic on this stretch.

If you are sharp-eyed, you can spot a stone marker for the Putney Fort, a structure built in 1755, replacing an earlier fort erected on the Great Meadows in 1744. The marker is just opposite a farm road that goes under the railroad track (mile 2.7) and just before Miller Road.

At mile 4.4, you can get a nice look at the river and on the

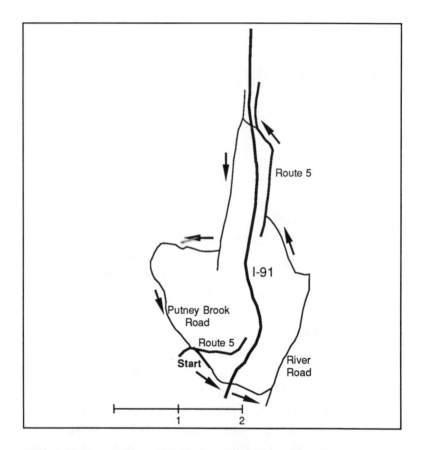

far side, the extensive cornfields in the floodplain. You also will come to the first climb, a relatively easy one of a quarter mile.

At mile 4.7, you will intersect Route 5. Turn right and carefully proceed north. There is little room for bikes on this section so be alert for traffic. Let the bike roll on the long downhill and then you will have one short uphill climb, with a narrow bike lane, before coming to the left turn at mile 6.2. Pedal under the interstate once more and you will immediately come to a dirt road running north/south. Turn sharp left and head up the hill. This will be a long climb of over a mile and then a level section of a mile. As you come down a shallow dip at mile 8.7, watch for a right turn onto Quarry Road.

Take Quarry Road and climb on the narrow dirt road. Notice the old stone walls and the large pine trees as you climb, fairly steeply at times. At mile 9.6, the road starts down in a sharp little turn and you will see a number of interesting metal modern art pieces scattered in the fields, the work of the artist whose studio you just pedaled past. One never knows what to expect on the back roads of Southern Vermont.

Continue downhill to a junction by a farm/junkyard at mile 10. Bear to the left down the hill to the intersection with Putney Brook Road. Turn left on Putney Brook Road and follow the brook back to your car.

Modern sculpture near the end
of the River Road Ride

Southwestern Routes

Arlington Loops
>Arlington Mt. Loop (*16.5 Miles Class 3*)
>Battenkill River Tour (*12 Miles Class 1*)

Bennington Loop (*13 Miles   Class 3*)
Shaftsbury Loop (*16 Miles Class 1*)
Somerset Rides
>Kelley Stand Ride (*32 Miles Class 1*)
>Pine Valley Loop (*18.5 Miles   Class 4*)
>Somerset Reservoir (*19 Miles Class 1*)

Stamford Klondike Ride (*13.5 Miles Class 3*)
West Rupert Railroad (*18 Miles Class 3*)
Woodford Stage Coach (*15 Miles Class 4*)

ARLINGTON LOOPS

Arlington, located on Historic Route 7A, is one of Vermont's tourist attractions. Known as the home of illustrator Norman Rockwell, the Village also is "home" to the Battenkill River, a famous trout stream. Arlington is located 14 miles north of Bennington and 9 miles south of Manchester.

Arlington Mountain Loop (16.5 Miles Class 3)

Short Summary
After an easy start along the River Road for a warmup and a climb on pavement, there's a difficult two mile climb on a dirt road/jeep trail followed by a steep descent. A hilly cutoff route on the return gets you off Route 7A. This is for riders who are in condition and want a unique climbing experience.

Directions To Start
From the center of Arlington on Route 7A, take Route 313 west toward Cambridge, New York. In less than a quarter mile, just before you pass over the Battenkill, there is a parking lot on the right side, adjacent to a golf course fairway. Except for opening day of trout season, there should be plenty of parking room.

Full Description

From the parking area, turn right on Route 313. Use care since this is a heavily traveled road. After less than a half mile, cross the highway and take the left by the Battenkill Canoe Rentals barn, cross the river, and turn right once you pedal over the small bridge. This is River Road (unmarked) which you will follow for the next 5.5 miles. The Battenkill, one of the premier trout streams in the Northeast, flows into New York state. All during trout season (second Saturday in April through October), you'll see fly fisherman casting in this lovely river. It is also a popular stream for canoeing.

As you start west on dirt, stay on the right branch of the road at mile .6 and proceed along the river. You'll pass the Four Winds Country Inn (802-375-6734) as you traverse the first stretch with the river off to your right. This is easy riding with plenty of places to stop and watch the water. Pass by the Benedict Hollow Road which climbs uphill and pedal on, enjoying the rolling terrain. (Mile 2.2)

The next half mile has some easy climbing and a short steep section, then a pleasant downhill. Notice how close the sugar maples, planted in the days of horses, are to the road, presenting quite a challenge for snow plow and school bus drivers these days. You'll ride into an open area with a horse farm before coming to the Inn On Covered Bridge Green, a former Norman Rockwell home (802-375-9489), at mile 4. Turn right and take a look at the Battenkill church and grange and the small covered bridge. This is a favorite stopping point of cycle groups coming down Route 313 as well as auto tourist — one of the most-photographed bridges in the state.

Cross through the covered bridge and turn right on Route 313 back towards Arlington. You'll pedal less than a half mile on this road but watch for traffic since there's not much room on the side. Turn left on the paved road that heads uphill towards Sandgate. This is Swearing Hill which reportedly got its name when two hunters claimed to have shot the same deer — back in 1761. You too may be swearing before this climb is over!

Mountain roads get quite rough in the spring

It is a steady climb on pavement to mile 5.9 when the road levels. As you pedal along, you can see some large hills up ahead — a taste of things to come. At mile 6.3, there's a row of tired-looking mailboxes on the right as well as a rusted road sign marked "So. East Corner." Turn right, cross the brook and get ready for some uphill riding.

The dirt road starts off easily for about a half mile and then, at mile 7, you will begin climbing for real. There are a number of camps and homes along the road but as you climb, notice how they become fewer and how the road begins to narrow. At mile 8, you will come to a sharp right turn and a steep climb. It is "granny gear" or push from here to the top of the climb at mile 8.9. What a monster uphill.

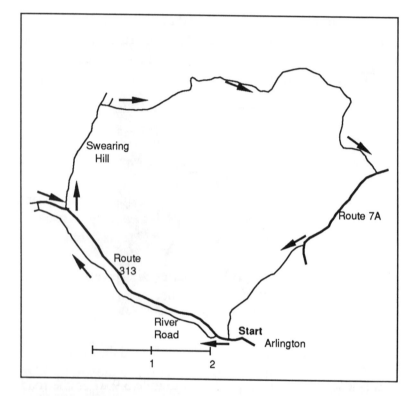

Don't worry about all the "No Trespassing" signs posted — they apply to the lands on either side of the road. This is a Class 4 road, a trail, that is a public right-of-way and perfect for mountain biking. The trail pitches down steeply and then levels off as you start passing the property owned by the Carthusian Foundation, the group that has the large monastery on Mount Equinox off to the north. You'll encounter some nice riding as well as some rough spots before heading downhill for real. There's a lot of altitude to lose before Route 7A.

The descent is steep and marked by vistas of the Green Mountain range across the valley. At mile 11, you drop down a narrow farm lane lined with sugar maples until the trail goes back to a wider dirt road. The downhill is steep and winding with one spectacular view to the south towards Bennington. Keep your speed under control because the last downhill ends right at the main highway at mile 12.5.

Turn right and wend your way back towards Arlington. There is only a very narrow lane for riding and the traffic can be fierce so take your time. After 1.3 miles on pavement, you will pass a road to the right called Red Mountain and right afterwards, Fisher Road. The next road, Tory Road, is a cutoff at mile 14. (Arlington was a nest of Tory sympathizers before and during the Revolution.) You now have a choice — you can continue on 7A or take the dirt road which has some more climbing.

Tory Road climbs steeply for a quarter mile, levels some, and then climbs sharply again. After a mile, the road converts to a trail as it starts downhill. It continues as a jeep trail until you approach Route 313 where it opens up and has a series of homes lining it. Turn left on the paved road and pedal the quarter mile back to the car. (If you chose to return down Route 7A, the bike lane is very limited. Turn right on Route 313 in the middle of Arlington to return to the parking area.

Battenkill River Tour (12 Miles   Class 1)

Short Summary
An out and back route on one of the easiest dirt road rides in Southern Vermont. Rolling, flat terrain along a pretty river with many photo and picnic sites.

Directions To Start
From the center of Arlington on Route 7A, take Route 313 west toward Cambridge, New York. In less than a quarter mile, just before you pass over the Battenkill, there is a parking lot on the right side, adjacent to a golf course fairway. Except for opening day of trout season, there should be plenty of parking.

Full Description
From the parking area, turn right on Route 313. Use care since this is a heavily traveled road. After less than a half mile, cross the highway and take the left by the Battenkill Canoe Rentals barn, cross the river, and turn right once you pedal over the small bridge. This is River Road (unmarked) which you will follow for the next 5.5 miles. The Battenkill, one of the premier trout streams in the Northeast, flows into New York state. All during trout season (second Saturday in April through October), you'll see fly fisherman casting in this lovely river.

As you start west on dirt, stay to the right at the first branch and proceed along the river. (Mile .6) You'll pass the Four Winds Country Inn (802-375-6734) as you traverse the first stretch with the river off to your right. This is easy riding with

Stay well to the right when riding on dirt roads

plenty of places to stop and watch the water. Pass by the Benedict Hollow Road which climbs uphill and pedal on, enjoying the rolling terrain. (Mile 2.2)

The next half mile has some easy climbing and a short steep section, then a pleasant downhill. Notice how close the sugar maples, planted in the era of horses, are to the road. They present quite a challenge these days for snow plow and school bus drivers. You'll ride into an open area with a horse farm before coming to the Inn On Covered Bridge Green, a former Norman Rockwell home (802-375-9489), at mile 4. Turn right

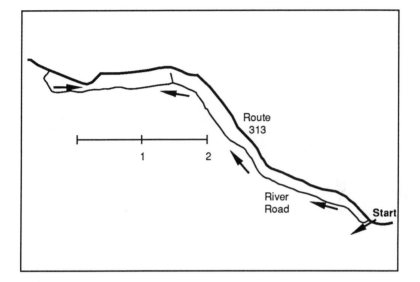

and take a look at the Battenkill church and grange and the small covered bridge. This is a favorite stopping point of cycle groups coming down Route 313 as well as auto tourists — one of the most-photographed bridges in the state.

Return to the river road and head west for another two miles of nice countryside riding. Remember that this road is used by many tourists so be alert for traffic. At mile 6, you'll come to a new bridge that crosses to Route 313. This is the turn point so when you are ready, retrace your route back to Arlington for some more gentle fat-tired cruising.

Bennington Loop (13 Miles   Class 3)

Short Summary

A ride 'round Mt. Anthony. Some steady climbing on rocky jeep trails. Spectacular views from several points and a long steep descent on pavement back to the start.

Directions To Start

Bennington is at the intersection of Routes 9 and 7. Old Bennington is just west on Route 9. As you climb the hill and swing left, there is ample parking near the Old First Church.

Full Description

Start out heading west, past the old Walloomsac Inn, on busy Route 9. As soon as the state highway starts, there is a wide bike lane as you pedal up a slight grade. Climb past the airport turn (.8 miles) and keep straight ahead until you see the sign for Fairdale Farms. This working dairy operates a snack bar noted for homemade ice cream. Perhaps you'll want to return after the ride. Turn left on Mt. Anthony Road and begin climbing.

This will be a challenging ride. I asked a Vermonter working in his garden about the route. He replied, "Yeh, keep taking left turns and you'll stay on dirt all the way to Monument Avenue. It will be a great ride ... unless it kills you!" He chuckled and went back to his weeding as I went back to my uphill pedalling.

The paved road goes to dirt at mile 1.8. There are nice views behind you and off to the west. After two miles of mostly up, a great downhill begins. The view unfolds as you descend.

There are fewer trees and more pasture as the road gets lower
— it is lovely riding.

After a series of downhills, you will come to a road going off
to the left sharply at mile 5.2. Be ready for it. Turn left, enjoying
a level stretch with some nice mountain scenery off to your
right. There's a downgrade before you pass a contractor's
building on a sweeping left turn. At the dirt intersection at mile
6.5, pedal straight ahead onto the trail. This will be rough for
about half a mile. You will pass under the power line and have
to negotiate some rocky terrain. The jeep trail starts to improve
as you climb through a stand of beech trees and at mile 7.1,
opens up to a large upland pasture with a lovely home at the top.
Yes, that narrow path straight ahead uphill is the route. It is a
half mile climb on the rocky path to the top of the hill. If
visibility is good, you will be rewarded with a truly spectacular view back to the west — take a moment to enjoy it.

At mile 7.6, the dirt road improves and after a half mile of
easy riding, you may be surprised to pass a migrant labor camp.
This facility serves the large orchard up ahead. At mile 8.4 there
will be one last steep climb ending at the Southern Vermont Orchards. Another spectacular vista opens to the south. If the
weather is clear, you can easily spot Mt. Greylock, the highest
mountain in Massachusetts. Just ahead is an intersection which
calls for a left turn back toward Bennington.

The road starts down steeply on dirt. The whole Bennington
area opens up before you as you come downhill — it is a
Vermont Life view with the battle monument as a centerpiece.
You'll coast on to new pavement down past an orchard and after
a wonderful downhill run, come to Route 7. Take a sharp left at
the intersection onto Monument Avenue.

The trip back to the car is through rural residential areas.
After a final coast down into Old Bennington you may want to

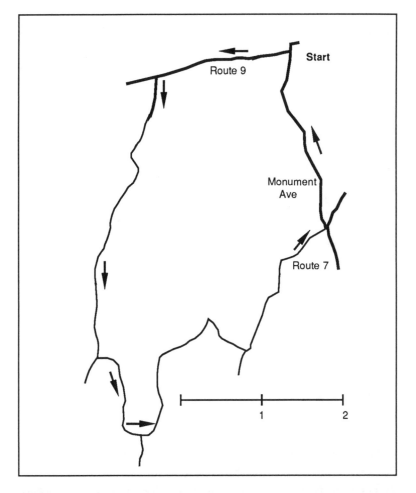

continue on Monument Avenue to the site of the Catamount Tavern, the gathering spot for the Green Mountain Boys, or pedal up to the 306 foot tall Bennington Battle Monument. Back at the church, the Burying Ground has the graves of many famous Vermonters, including five former governors and the poet Robert Frost. When you're ready, it may be time to check out the ice cream flavors at Fairdale Farms.

Shaftsbury Loop (16 Miles   Class 1)

Short Summary

An easy ride on rolling terrain with several excellent views and one short stretch of trail riding. A good ride for novices.

Directions To Start

From the south, take Route 7A north from Bennington past Shaftsbury Center. Look for a brown converted sheep barn called the Chocolate Barn (a place with hand-dipped chocolates for a post-ride snack). After a sweeping left turn on 7A, take Depot Road, the next paved road to the right. Park under the power line on the right hand side, about 200 yards from the main highway. There's room for 3-4 autos.

From the north, take Route 7A south from Manchester, through Arlington, and head south, past the Shaftsbury State Park. Depot Road is a left turn 1.3 miles south of the park.

Full Description

Head northeast on Depot Road, passing Dexter Road on your right (that is where the route finishes). The road changes to dirt as you cross the railroad tracks so enjoy some level riding with mountain ranges on both sides of the route. You will pass the intersection with Maple Hill and after a mile, come to a bog. This is nice easy pedaling on a smooth road as you parallel Warm Brook. There are some pretty views of the mountains north of Arlington. The small body of water up ahead is Miller's Pond. After passing Whimsey Farm B & B (802-375-6654), you will cross the railroad track once more (this is an active line, so don't be surprised to see a freight train heading up to Mack Moulding in Arlington) and intersect Route 7A at mile 3.

You just have to ride up around the corner on the main highway, less than a quarter mile, so do it with care since there's not much of a shoulder. Turn right at the paved road marked "Warm Brook Road" and proceed on pavement to the first right, Maple Hill Road. There is also a sign for Peter Matteson Tavern.

So far, the route has been easy riding with a little more pavement than you need for a mountain bike tour. If you look up ahead, you can see that things are about to change — the road changes to dirt and heads uphill. This will be a modest climb. Stay on Maple Hill Road and continue climbing. You will ascend until mile 4.4 and then, after a level stretch for a breather, continue the climb up a moderate incline. Mountain bikes eat these little hills up. There's over a mile of easy back road riding through this next section. At mile 6, note the well-manicured Christmas tree plantation. At mile 6.6, you will come to a short downhill with a fork in the road. Take the left called East Road. (Potter Montgomery Road goes to the right.)

As you coast through the intersection, you'll see a cemetery on the left. Because of all the tourist traffic in the area, it is fenced in. Climb up the small hill, pass the Glastenbury Road on the left (a little loop for future exploration) and at mile 7.6, you be at the historic Peter Matteson Tavern. Matteson built the place in about 1780 and in addition to being a farmer, ran a tavern as well. It is easy to imagine early travelers stopping for a pint of ale as they traversed this early stage coach road. You can stop and check out some of the restored facility, or can take a swig from your water bottle and press on up the hill on your knobby-tired steed.

The road starts up on the steepest climb of this loop — about .4 miles in length. On top, you get a great close-up view of the rugged Glastenbury Mountain. (The Appalachian Trail goes along that crest.) You will immediately come to a half mile downhill that is straight and gentle so let 'er rip. As the road goes back to pavement, note that the new Route 7 is just off to the left.

A beaver pond is a nice place to stop and relax

Just before you cross under Route 7, at mile 10, take the right turn on the dirt road (unmarked). This is Holy Smoke Road. Climb up to the corner and enjoy a lovely pastoral view to the north. After a half mile, the road turns right and pitches downhill. This is steep and narrow and made more interesting by a series of diagonal water barriers cut into the road to ease erosion. There is also an interesting mix of expensive new homes and house trailers along the way.

At mile 11.3, you will come to a "T" intersection. Take the left turn and watch for traffic — this is travelled more frequently. A long downhill run past a horse farm followed by a straight run out will bring you, at mile 12.3, to Hollow Road, a

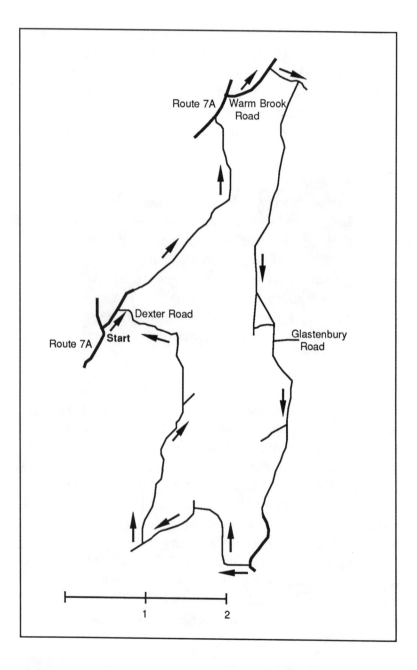

Route 7A   Warm Brook Road

Dexter Road

Route 7A   **Start**

Glastenbury Road

1   2

sharp right turn. If you cross the railroad, you have gone too far.

Watch out for trucks along this section. The road is flat and wide and oiled to keep the dust down since dump trucks haul gravel continually during the week from a massive gravel pit just up ahead. At mile 12.6, you will pass a beaver dam and be able to see the railroad tracks on the far bank. This is smooth riding among the tamarack trees. At mile 13, ignore the turn to the left, that's the gravel pit, and head up the hill. No more trucks up here.

As you climb, you can see the extensive gravel operation. Pass by the Clement Greene Road on the right and then at mile 14, turn off Hollow Road to Dexter Road. Go straight ahead on the road that soon will turn to a trail. There are a couple of interesting new homes until the road goes to a jeep trail. This stretch may look private but it is a public trail. The terrain is easy except for a couple of rocky sections. There is a house trailer that you will pass as you climb up toward an intersection. Take the road to the left that goes down the hill and at mile 15, you'll pass a restored farmhouse as the road opens up again. It is an easy ride, with one neat downhill, back to the intersection with Depot Road. Turn left and there's the car. Perhaps it is time to check out the Chocolate Barn.

SOMERSET RIDES

The Somerset/Stratton area has long been a favorite of hunters and hikers. Now it has become a mecca for mountain bike riders. Most of the land is either Green Mountain National Forest or owned by the New England Power Company. It has a network of roads and trails that track for miles in this relatively remote area of the state. Because of easier access, this area has more visitors each year and is losing some of the unspoiled nature it once enjoyed. The Kelly Stand ride is a good example, following a long Forest Service road that was not finished until the last few years. The Somerset area just begs you to get a group together and explore it by bike. Here are two easy rides and one more challenging one to give you a taste of the area.

Kelly Stand (32 Miles   Class 1)

Short Summary
A long out-and-back ride to the Kelly Stand Road. Primarily level riding suited for riders of mixed abilities. The ride can be shortened by having a driver go on ahead, leave a vehicle at the Kelly Stand parking area, and then pedal back to meet you.

Directions To Start
The turn for Somerset is at the foot of Searsburg Mountain on Route 9 just 5.4 miles west of Wilmington or 15.5 miles east of Bennington. There is parking on both sides of the road just off Route 9 on the paved Somerset Road.

Full Description

Head north on the paved road (which is old Route 9) which will soon go to dirt at mile .2. The large black conduit snaking down the valley on your right carries water to the New England Power Company generating facilities. Because of the diversion of flow, the river bed will usually be quite dry in this section of your route. After a mile, you will pedal past the dam and cruise around the impoundment lined with yellow and white birch trees. There are some pretty views to the north — much of that land is owned by NEPCO.

You've got four miles of gentle riding ahead as you follow the course of the Deerfield River upstream. Expect traffic on this road since it is popular with folks who boat on Somerset Reservoir and is a route to the Stratton recreational areas. With the smooth dirt conditions, cars whip along at 30 mph or more, so stay alert. At mile 2 you will pedal past the suspension foot bridge that crosses the river. This is the hiking trail to Somerset Reservoir. Shortly thereafter, the road passes several private camps and a cemetery. You will enter the Green Mountain National Forest at mile 4 and start the first easy climb. This is an area with many side roads and trails. Note the interesting ones for future exploration. For example, after crossing Rake Brook, you will see the gated road heading off to the west which gives way to a forest trail.

After some gentle climbs, you will come upon another Forest Service road marked "325 — Road Closed" just before you cross the river at mile 6. (This is the turn for the Pine Valley Ride.) At mile 6.2, you will come to an intersection with the right fork heading up the hill to the reservoir and the left marked "Somerset Airport." Take the left fork, Forest Service Road 71.

The road narrows at once as it goes past a series of picnic area and primitive camping sites. This area is known as "the airport"

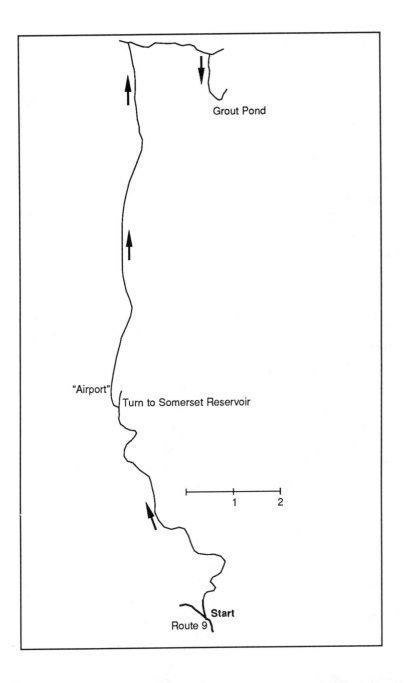

Grout Pond

"Airport"

Turn to Somerset Reservoir

1   2

Start

Route 9

due to the fact that there was a small airfield here during the logging operations of the 1940s. You will have level riding through an area of pine trees. All through this stretch, there are side roads that just demand exploring by mountain bike. Right away, you'll spot one going off to the left, through the river, and if the day is hot, you might want to try out your "fording the creek" technique before proceeding on.

There are several miles of easy riding with some easy climbs on the narrow road. At mile 7.5 you'll encounter the first uphill of any significance, but it lasts only for a quarter of a mile. As you pedal along, notice the number of well-formed spruce trees that have seeded themselves along the road bank where they can compete for moisture and light.

At mile 8.4, you'll come to an intersection where Forest Road 83 heads off to the left. It is another road marked "Dead End" which applies to motor vehicles. This is an active snow-mobile route in the winter and connects with FR 192 which eventually, after passing a shelter, returns to FR 71, the road you are taking. Go straight ahead following the sign marked "Stratton."

There's a pretty bog, Shep Meadows, surrounded by ever-greens on your left at mile 9, and shortly thereafter, the road will climb moderately for nearly half a mile. Through breaks in the trees, there are some nice views of the Glastenbury area to the west.

The first downhill comes at mile 9.8 and is gentle and straight, lasting for only .3 miles. You will come to an area of hardwoods which has been logged and start descending again. This will be a long winding descent making up for the gradual climbing that you've done for the last 10 miles. At mile 12.8, you will pass a road coming in from the right, one of the many trails and roads that link up with the fingers of Somerset

Reservoir. After some gentle climbs and descents, you will start down and find that the road steepens as you coast to the Kelly Stand Road (Forest Highway 6) at mile 14.8. Turn right and proceed, watching for auto traffic.

There are a number of things that can be done at this point. The Long Trail/Appalachian Trail crosses just down the road and trying to ride on that is one thing not to do. Not only is it impossible due to rough terrain, it also is a good way to get mountain bike riding restricted in this area.

You might want to check out the Daniel Webster monument and shelter. Back in the 1800s, this road, the Stratton Turnpike, was a popular way to get to the famed waters and hotels of Saratoga Springs. In 1840, the famed orator Daniel Webster made a campaign speech on behalf of the Whig ticket of Harrison and Tyler to a large crowd (10,000 to 20,000). Things haven't ever been as lively on this side of Stratton Mountain since.

If you pedal east, you'll pass the large parking area for Kelly Stand and can take FR 262 to the right down to Grout Pond. This popular body of water has recently had an improved access road and picnic areas added by the Forest Service. As you will note, this whole area has been made more attractive to visitors and is becoming crowded, thus becoming less suited for mountain biking — until you get off the beaten paths.

The return ride will retrace your route. After a couple of difficult climbs from the Kelly Stand Road, it will be generally downhill. Be sure to give yourself plenty of time to get back before dusk since it is 15 miles back to the car.

Pine Valley (18.5 Miles   Class 4)

Short Summary

A good taste of backwoods mountain biking. One third of this ride is easy dirt road, one-third technically-challenging, and one-third paved highway. Plan to carry water, snacks, and a Woodford U.S.G.S topographic map with you.

Directions To Start

The turn for Somerset is at the foot of Searsburg Mountain on Route 9 just 5.4 miles west of Wilmington or 15.5 miles east of Bennington. There is parking on both sides of the road just off Route 9 on the paved Somerset Road.

Full Description

Head north on the paved road (which is old Route 9) which will soon go to dirt at mile .2. The large black conduit snaking down the valley on your right carries water to the New England Power Company generating facilities. Because of the diversion of flow, the river bed will usually be quite dry in this section of your route. After a mile, you will pedal past the dam and cruise around the impoundment lined with yellow and white birch trees. There are some pretty views to the north.

You've got four miles of gentle riding ahead as you follow the course of the Deerfield River upstream. Expect traffic on this road since it is popular with folks who boat on Somerset Reservoir and is a route to the Stratton recreational areas. With the smooth dirt conditions, cars whip along at 30 mph or more, so stay alert. At mile 2 you will pedal past the suspension foot bridge that crosses the river. This is the hiking trail to Somerset Reservoir. Shortly thereafter, the road passes several private camps and a cemetery. You will enter the Green Mountain National Forest at mile 4 and start the first easy climb. This is an area with many side roads and trails. Note the interesting ones for future exploration. For example, after crossing Rake Brook you will see the gated road heading off to the west which gives way to a forest trail.

At mile 5.9, after some gentle climbs, you will come upon Forest Service Road 325 marked "Road Closed." Turn left and cruise up this flat road that follows the tannic-acid colored Castle Brook. This is part of Corridor 7, a major snowmobile route, and is called the Glastenbury Road by some since it takes winter riders to Glastenbury Mountain. After a half mile of easy riding, you will cross the brook and start climbing gently up to a beaver pond and bog. If the beavers are active and plugging culverts, you may find the road flooded. Pedalling on, you will pass a metal gate and, at mile 7.2, go by a trail that goes off to the left. That is the old Corridor 7 trail and the bridge has been removed. Proceed straight ahead and as the road climbs to the right, you'll see the well-marked Corridor 7 trail ahead. The sign says "Corridor 7S — Woodford 9 miles."

Get psyched for some challenging riding. This is the type of trail where you spend a lot of time carrying the bike or hopping off and back on it. There are many rocky spots and boggy areas — great mountain bike terrain. Head straight, following the signs with a green diamond (marking a major snowmobile route). Right away, you will face the obstacle of a rock-strewn approach to a wooden snowmobile bridge over the creek. This structure is typical of those you will find on this route — the trail is well-maintained by snowmobile club members who work

Saturdays through the summer clearing debris and constructing stream crossings such as this.

Beavers often flood parts of the Pine Valley route

As you proceed, you may notice that this trail is not well-marked but is wide and easily discernable. Watch for little jewels of ponds surrounded by stark dead trees as you go along. After just over a half mile of slow going, you will come to a clearing. The old trail, blocked off, goes straight ahead. You will want to take a sharp right as shown by an arrow. This is much easier riding since it is a much older and more-developed trail. On your left is the large Castle Meadows bog. This whole area, as you know by now, is laced with tiny streams and acres of swamps and bogs. You half expect to encounter a moose.

At mile 9.5, Corridor 7 swings south and you will have two miles of technical riding with plenty of spots to carry the bike. For riders interested in trials riding, this is a blast. Each snowmobile bridge is a challenge. Try to get the front wheel up

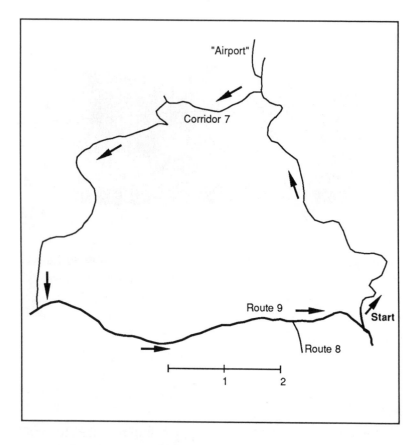

on it and then ride across. At last, the riding, as you pick up the Pine Valley Road, is easier. Pine Valley starts at a major snowmobile trail intersection and proceeds south, climbing up to a large parking area on Route 9. (Some mountain bikers start here and ride to the airport area on the Somerset Road, but in a few miles, when you scream down Searsburg Mountain, you'll be glad that you went in this direction.)

You now are faced with 5 miles of riding on the shoulder of Route 9. The shoulder is narrow in spots and there is lots of

One of the many bogs along the way

traffic so take it easy and use those fat tires to stay as far as possible off the highway. What a contrast from the wilderness riding you just finished. Just after the Woodford State Park, you will roll down an incline and come to the Twin Brook General Store (802-442-4054), also known as "The Woodford Mall." This is a great place to grab some nourishment, including grinders, as well as information on local roads and trails. The patrons are active snowmobilers and know the area well. They are very hospitable to mountain bike riders.

After one last climb to Searsburg, you will pass the Route 8 turn and have a wonderful long downhill to your car. The road has a nice wide bike lane, so enjoy this easy ending to a challenging ride.

Somerset Reservoir (19 Miles   Class 1)

Short Summary

An out-and-back ride to the Somerset Reservoir picnic site. Primarily level riding suited for riders of mixed abilities. One long climb going to and leaving the reservoir.

Directions To Start

The turn for Somerset is at the foot of Searsburg Mountain on Route 9 just 5.4 miles west of Wilmington or 15.5 miles east of Bennington. There is parking on both sides of the road just off Route 9 on the paved Somerset Road.

Full Description

Head north on the paved road (which is old Route 9) which will soon go to dirt at mile .2. The large black conduit snaking down the valley on your right carries water to the New England Power Company generating facilities. Because of the diversion of flow, the river bed will usually be quite dry in this section of your route. After a mile, you will pedal past the dam and cruise around the impoundment lined with yellow and white birch trees. There are some pretty views to the north.

You've got four miles of gentle riding ahead as you follow the course of the Deerfield River upstream. Expect traffic on this road since it is popular with folks who boat on Somerset Reservoir and is a route to the Stratton recreational areas. With the smooth dirt conditions, cars whip along at 30 mph or more, so stay alert. At mile 2 you will pedal past the suspension foot bridge that crosses the river. This is the hiking trail to Somerset Reservoir. Shortly thereafter, the road passes several private camps and a cemetery. You will enter the Green Mountain National Forest at mile 4 and start the first easy climb. This is an area with many side roads and trails. Note the interesting ones for future exploration. For example, after crossing Rake Brook you will see the gated road heading off to the west which gives way to a forest trail.

After some gentle climbs, you will come upon another Forest Service road marked "325 — Road Closed" just before you cross the river at mile 6. (This is the turn for the Pine Valley Ride.) At mile 6.2, you will come to an intersection with the right fork heading up the hill to the reservoir and the left marked "Somerset Airport." This area is known by that name due to the fact that just ahead there was a small airfield during the logging operations of the 1940s. Take the right fork to go to the reservoir.

It is quite a little climb up from the intersection, especially in terms of the easy riding you have had so far. Note the old apple trees along the road — this was once farm country. After a quarter mile of uphill, you will come upon an enclave of private hunting camps. Just as the road swings right, you will note a spring flowing into a barrel — a good place to stop and refill water bottles. Continue climbing, steeply at times, and as you top the rise a mile 7.5, there will be several more camps on your left and a pretty upland pasture on your right. The mountain ahead is the back side of Mount Snow.

Get ready for a great downhill. As you descend for nearly a half mile, the dam should be visible through the trees straight ahead. The road levels and after a mile of rolling terrain, you will be at the face of the impoundment. There is a stairway to the top but if you pedal along the base and continue to the east

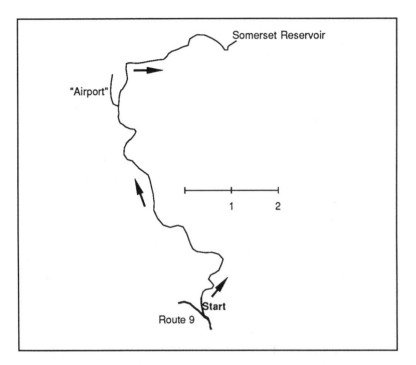

side, the road loops around and you can climb to the top of the dam where there is a nice spot to stop (mile 9.5). That's Glastenbury Mountain off to the west and Stratton Mountain straight ahead. If you pedal up the road there will be a large picnic area along the lake with some pretty spots in the shade to stop and relax.

The return leg has one tough long climb two miles from the reservoir but then it is downhill to the intersection. If you have time, turn right at the "airport" junction and pedal north for a bit, checking out the primitive camping sites and side trails for future expeditions. It is just over six miles back to the start and the route, since it follows the river downstream, is a gentle descent on a smooth road.

Stamford Klondike Ride (13.5 Miles   Class 3)

Short Summary

A steep climb of 3 miles into the Green Mountain range followed by a loop on back roads with two crossings of the Appalachian Trail. Ends with a long descent back to Stamford. Some technically-demanding riding and fairly steep climbing.

Directions To Start

Start in the middle of Stamford. Parking is available at the school/town office complex or if mid-week, at the two churches. From Route 9 in Searsburg, take Route 8 south for 13.8 miles to Stamford. From North Adams, take Route 2 east and Route 8 north. (5.5 miles) There is a convenience store just to the south of the parking site.

Full Description

Pedal north to Mill Street and turn left, heading west on pavement as it heads out of town along Roaring Branch Brook. This will be a nice warmup for the hill that you can see ahead. The road goes to dirt by the town garage and starts climbing along the pretty brook. The hills rise sharply on both sides of you as you climb, steeply at times. Be alert for traffic — there are some narrow spots ahead. At mile 1.2 there will be a road jutting off to the right and a half mile later, a very steep uphill as the road crosses the brook several times. At mile 1.8, you'll spot the Roaring Branch Trail heading north. This is an active snowmobile trail in the winter, connecting with the Stage

Coach Road west of Heartwellville. (Perhaps a later exploration ride — it gets pretty rough after a few miles.)

Continue uphill steeply for another quarter mile. This is
tough climbing — you may have to do some pushing — but it
is almost over. As you approach several new homes, the road
levels for a bit before starting up again. Maltese Road goes off
to the right at mile 2.6. You should continue straight ahead.

The road changes to more of a jeep trail at mile 3.3 as you
continue to climb. These roads are rough but kept open by the
town to provide access to hikers on the Long Trail in case of
emergency. You will see evidence of grading and rough drain-
age work as you pedal. There's lots of water so expect some
muddy sections up ahead.

The climbing is easier as you pedal through an area flanked
by an old stone wall with a smattering of birch trees mixed in
with the hardwoods. At mile 4, Klondike Road, unmarked,
comes up from the south — you will be returning on that. Press
on straight ahead. As you come to the top of the rise, peer
through the trees to your left and you can see Mt. Greylock near
North Adams. At mile 4.8 you will see the sign for the Long
Trail/Appalachian Trail crossing and then, after the power line,
you'll start down. This is a great mountain bike descent —
rocky with small streams running in the middle of the road. At
the bottom, the left turn is your route. This road, which you'll
love, is called Risky Ranch Road. (The trail straight ahead ends
up in Pownal Center on Route 7 — a nice ride if you can figure
how to get back to your car.)

Most of the year, you will encounter a lot of water in pools
and streamlets as you pedal this flat section of road. The Long
Trail again crosses at mile 5.7 but is difficult to pick out. There's
not much to see in this back road stretch which is forested with
northern hardwoods, primarily beech trees. This changes at

mile 6.3 when you pass a camp and start an easy climb past an old pasture lined with apple trees. At the top of the short climb, you'll pass a camp marked "The Little White House" and, as the road widens, start on a great downhill. There's a mile and a half of easy descending so let the bike run. After crossing the brook twice, you'll come to the intersection of Klondike and pay for all the fun you just had. Turn left and prepare to climb.

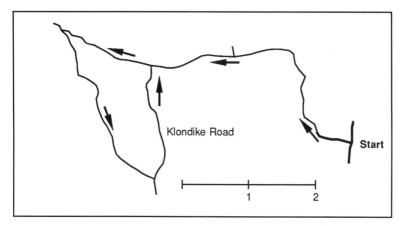

As you start down the hill across the bridge, get ready for an immediate steep climb by downshifting early. You will grunt up past an old farm (whose noisy dogs were tied) and continue up past some lovely upland pastures. The uphills are fairly easy with some level spots. At mile 8.6 there will be a summer home on the right with a road leading past it back towards Stamford.

Klondike Road is well-named — the next section is rough and wet and steep. It is a mile of tough going until you come to the intersection with Mill Road. From the intersection, turn right and there will be an immediate descent. There's nothing but downhill all the way back to Stamford. Why not find a spot near one of the deep pools of the brook and stop for a rest? It has been a short but challenging ride.

West Rupert Railroad (18 Miles   Class 3)

Short Summary

Starting with an easy ride along a deserted railroad bed, the route then climbs a long steep dirt road/trail. A short descent is followed by about ten miles of back road riding with several challenging uphills. This is an interesting trip through Bennington County hill farm and slate quarry countryside.

Directions To Start

West Rupert is just over a mile from the New York border. From the Saratoga area, take Route 29 to Route 22 to Salem, then Route 153 to W. Rupert (27 miles). From Manchester, Vermont, take Route 30 through Dorset, Route 315 to Rupert, and Route 153 to W. Rupert (15 miles). Take Mill Road, just north of the Post Office, west past Authentic Designs, a lighting fixture business, and park opposite the Town Clerk's office so that you are well off the road. The railroad bed is just to the west.

Full Description

The ride begins on the stretch of railroad bed that once was the Delaware & Hudson Railroad. This property has been acquired by the State of Vermont and is managed by the Department of Forest, Parks, & Recreation (802-244-8711) for use as a hiking, biking, and cross country ski trail. It runs from West Rupert all the way to Castleton (34 miles) weaving into New York for 14 miles as it heads north. You will ride it for the next six miles. The railroad bed is as flat a mountain bike trail as you will find in Vermont but the route offers scenes that makes it easy to imagine being seated behind an old steam locomotive. Pedalling through canopies of leaves, one can visualize the leaves swaying from the exhaust plume. But enough nostalgia, let's pedal. All aboard!

As you begin on the West Rupert to Rupert stretch of rail bed,

The Rupert Depot Station and bike path

you'll be riding just to the west of Route 153 for a little over a mile. When you cross the Hebron Road crossing at mile 1.2, you should spot the spire of the church in Rupert. Next, you'll see the Rupert Depot building at mile 1.5.

Leaving Rupert heading north, there will be a number of corn fields on both sides of the route. The cinder base of the road bed is soft and a little slow in this section — you'll need to ride in a slightly lower gear then on a dirt road. As you pedal along, there will be similarities to riding on a train. You'll see a different perspective of Vermont — the back side of barns that sometimes aren't painted, the back side of houses, the backside of Holsteins. It's great riding.

Like most rural railroads, this one crosses back and forth across the road it parallels. Use caution as you come up on the road at mile 4.7. The concrete abutments from the old road straddle the trail at this point. Then you'll have a mile of easier

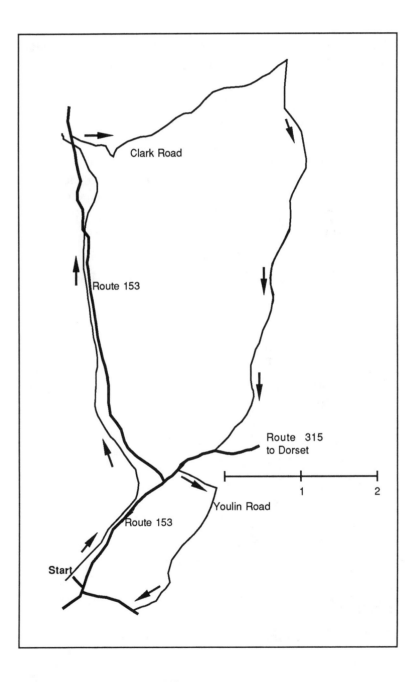

Clark Road

Route 153

Route 315
to Dorset

Youlin Road

1   2

Route 153

Start

pedaling since there is less cinder covering. As you come out of the wooded area into the open, be sure to notice the rock outcroppings in the pastures on the right. It is easy to see why this area has so many slate quarries.

There's a large red barn across the field on your left and a concrete bridge as you approach Route 153. This is where you will leave the railroad (The bike path continues ahead). Check for traffic and turn right, pedaling for a tenth of a mile to the dirt road that goes right (Clark Road — unmarked). The flat riding is over (mile 6.0). (Another day, you may want to explore more of the Delaware and Hudson route, going on to West Pawlet, Granville, New York, and points north on the line.)

You will start up at once and after a gradual start, face a steep quarter mile climb. Quite a change from the railroad, isn't it? As the climb lessens, catch your breath by noting the pretty hillside pastures on both sides of the road. If you look straight ahead uphill, you can see the hill you are going to climb. The road continues up for another mile, with some breathers and then some steep sections. At mile 7.5, the road converts to a trail but press on, there is some interesting riding just ahead. Here's where a mountain bike shows its stuff.

There's a camp on the right as the trail gets rockier and steeper. (This is a Class 4 trail, a public right-of-way.) You will have a bumpy half mile of climbing before the road levels off on top. When it does, pause for a moment and note the stone walls and birch trees. There are some lovely stands of white birch through this section.

The first downhill is a little rocky and steep and then descends in a nice half mile drop to an old farm site which is marked by old apple trees and a weathered barn. You will emerge from the woods at Jam Hill Farm where the trail changes back to a dirt road and where there is a spectacular view to the north. Check out the interesting geological formations. As you continue to descend, the road comes to an intersection. This is the old "Pawlet Mountain Turnpike", now known as Pawlet Mountain Road. (Mile 8.5)

Turn right on this smooth dirt surface and climb briefly before leveling off near a large dairy farm. After some easier riding, there will be an easy downhill and more level riding until you come to another dairy farm and a long hill. (Of course, you are going to climb it!) This will be a steady half mile uphill. Stop and look back at the view behind you as you climb.

The level riding on top ends with a long steep downhill to an intersection with Suncrest Road at mile 11.5. Pedal straight ahead and get ready for another long downhill to Route 315 (Mile 14.2). Be alert for farm machinery on this road — there are many manure spreaders, lime trucks, and silage wagons that use these roads. What a wonderful long downhill to Route 153.

At the intersection, turn right and pedal just a half mile to Youlin Road which climbs off to your left. (If you are ready to quit, continue down Route 153 to West Rupert.) As you can see, Youlin Road pitches up steeply. It is a tough climb but if you look back to the right, there's a nice view of Rupert. As soon as you reach the top, the narrow stone wall-lined road starts down again. Peek through the trees to see Antone Mountain to the left.

This is a long downhill passing through a major farm operation. You should see dozens of Ayrshire cattle in the fields along the way — this is one of the larger operations in the area. Since black & white Holsteins comprise over 90% of the state's dairy cattle, it is unusual to see so many brown and white cattle. At mile 17.3, you will come to the farm and an intersection. Turn right on the paved road and head back to West Rupert. Stop and have a snack at the Country Store — you have earned it.

Woodford Stage Coach (15 Miles Class 4)

Short Summary

An out-and-back route in the Green Mountain National Forest with some technically difficult riding on challenging trails. Mud, rocks, and steep climbs make this a ride for the experienced mountain bike rider. Plan to carry water, snacks, and a Stamford U.S.G.S topographic map with you.

Directions To Start

Start at Prospect Mountain Ski Area on Route 9. From Bennington, head east on Route 9 for 9 miles, climbing Woodford Mountain. From the east, take Route 9 from Wilmington for 13 miles, climbing Searsburg Mountain. From the south, take Route 8 or 100 north to Searsburg, then Route 9 west for 5 miles. Park just off Route 9 near the Vermont information display.

Full Description

Pedal west on Route 9 toward Bennington. (You can stay carefully on the left since the distance is short and there's a wide shoulder.) Just as you start down the steep hill, take the dirt road that goes off sharply to the left (.2 miles). The next few miles, you will be riding on a good dirt road recently built by the Forest Service for logging access.

Just after you start down on dirt, take the right that swings uphill sharply marked "273 Forest Road." You will level off at mile .5 and pass a number of Prospect Mountain cross country

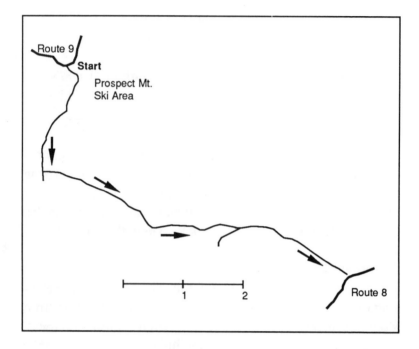

trails and snowmobile routes. Just ahead is a nice long downhill and a mile of twisting road — easy dirt road riding. If you look ahead through breaks in the trees, you can see the mountains that you'll be climbing. Stay on the main dirt road and enjoy some nice climbs and descents. You may see evidence of logging operations along here such as stored equipment or log piles since it serves as a staging area for operations up in the mountains.

At mile 2, you will start downhill and pedal past an intersection of logging trails and cross the Stamford Stream, barely noticeable at this altitude. After a steep climb through an area of recent logging, the road levels. If you are sharp-eyed, you can spot an orange property marker on the left, a signal to take the next left turn into what looks like a driveway. (Mile 2.5)

Take the left which will lead you to a private home (brown with a deck on the west side and a grey garage to the south). Get ready to climb.

This area has been disfigured by recent logging (1988/89) so the trail that you want, Forest Service Corridor 9, the Old Stage Coach Road, is difficult to pick out. It is right behind the garage of the private home and heads east up the mountain. Go to the right of the garage and then take a sharp left. There's a green arrow on a tree which marks the snowmobile trail. Walk your bike through the rubble for about 100 yards and you'll see the Stage Coach Road. It climbs the hill and has fairly large boulders along the way. It must have been some ride before balloon tires.

You will be flanking the George Aiken Wilderness Area, which lies to the north, as you climb. The Stage Coach Road starts up very steeply and is tricky climbing for a half mile. There are many washouts and rocky sections as well as sections scarred by logging equipment. At mile 3.5, you will get a reprieve from uphill and will be able to look down into the bog called Camp Meadows. There are also several nice mountain views through the trees to the north.

The next mile and a half is challenging mountain bike riding along an undulating jeep trail with rock outcrops, pools of stagnant muddy water, and if there has been recent logging, mud. At mile 5, you will start back down and have a rough rocky descent for a half mile until coming to a small gravel pit where the road opens up again. Be alert for vehicles from here on since the road is passable all the way to Route 8. The riding is easy compared to what you have just completed and after a mile, you will cross the West Branch of the Deerfield River on a sturdy Forest Service bridge. This may be a good time to stop and splash some water on your face — that was a good workout.

There are a couple of alternatives here before you retrace your route:

1. Continue on the Forest Service Road along the river to Heartwellville on Route 8. This is easy flat riding. I wish that I could tell you that there's a Ben & Jerry's Ice Cream Shop waiting for you in Heartwellville, but all you will find are a few houses and an old highway bridge (1929) across the West Branch of the Deerfield River. It is a nice spot to picnic before heading back.

The side trail to Yaw Pond
requires a lot of pushing

2. Take the Yaw Brook trail, a marked snowmobile trail, which goes off to the left just after the bridge. This path, which goes to Yaw Pond, is flat but quite difficult due to wetness and many rocks. You will push and carry the bike some during the three-quarter mile trek to Yaw Pond. The pond is shallow and boggy — interesting, but not your pristine swimming hole. (If you like wading and carrying mountain bikes through thickets of briars, you can continue north for two more very difficult miles on the snow machine trail. You will connect with Forest Service Road 74 which in turn brings you to Route 9, about 4 miles east of the starting point. This route is too rough and wet for mountain bike riding and is mainly mountain bike portaging.)

Grab a snack for the return trip because after an easy start, you've again got some tough riding ahead. The climb up to the gravel pit is easy riding but then, the trail upward is long and steep. If you take it easy, you should be able to ride all but the worst sections. The last downhill is fun, in spite of the roughness, because you know that easy riding lies ahead. Then it is a right turn after the brown house and a pleasant dirt road pedal. After some downhills, there's some climbing to do to get back to Route 9. Those downhills that were so much fun on the way in are now work for tired legs. As you pass the cross country trails, get ready for the last downhill — it is steep with a good left turn so enjoy it — you should be able to coast nearly to the highway. Your car is just up to the right.

West River Loops

Ball Mountain (*15 Miles Class 2*)
Pleasant Valley (*11.5 Miles Class 3*)
Turkey Mountain (*18 Miles Class 3*)
Weston Routes
        Hapgood Pond (*13 Miles Class 2*)
        Weston Priory (*13 miles Class 3*)
        Weston Short Loop (*8.5 Miles Class 3*)

Ball Mountain Loop (15 miles Class 2)

Short Summary

If you like pretty rides along rocky streams — this one's for you. Gradual climbs and a long descent mark the start and finish of this ride. The middle section has several steep climbs. For advanced beginners and accomplished riders.

Directions To Start

Jamaica is located 25.5 miles from Brattleboro on Route 30. If you are coming up Route 100, it is three miles west of the intersection of Route 100 and Route 30. In the center of Jamaica, turn left off Route 30 and stay on the right fork, South Hill Road. Track 2.3 miles from Route 30 until you come to an intersection with a good-sized bridge over Ball Mountain Brook. There is parking here for several cars.

Full Description

Begin the ride by taking the dirt road which heads up toward Pikes Falls. You'll start off on a smooth sandy road that wanders along the North Branch of the Ball Mountain Brook. This will be easy riding past some camps with just a few minor climbs. The road changes to pavement at mile 1.7. (Many of these back roads are being paved to accommodate skiers.)

Continuing on the paved road, you'll come across a small settlement known as Pikes Falls. This is a favorite local swimming hole — you can spot the trail leading off to the left down through the woods. Ignore all roads branching off; stay on the paved road. As you rolll down a slight grade and cross a small bridge over the North Branch, you can see the ski slopes of Stratton Mountain looming ahead. Keep pedaling on the level paved road watching for a left turn at mile 4. This is County Road and is marked with a green sign — it's a sharp left and immediate climb.

As you start up the narrow road, gear down and keep your weight distributed for traction. You'll have a steep climb on gravel for a half mile. After a brief respite and an all too brief downhill, there will be another climb to an intersection marked by a grey summer home. Take the right up the hill and be on the lookout for horses. This narrow "road", Stone Chimney Road, is a favorite riding trail as you may note from the hoof prints and droppings. After a rough climb of a quarter mile, the paved Stratton Mountain Road lies ahead. Turn left, keeping eyes and ears open for traffic.

Because of the proximity to Stratton, the Mountain Road can get a lot of traffic so be watchful — you will have about 3.5 miles of up and down riding on this road. Check your brakes and enjoy a steep downhill on smooth pavement for .5 miles. What a neat way to cool off after that last set of climbs. The road goes to dirt as you bottom out crossing Kidder Brook (mile 5.6) and then climb. What you see is what you get — a half mile uphill.

Catch a drink of water from your bottle on top where the road levels for a bit and get ready to whip down another great descent. Pass Forester Road and then Half Mile Road on the left and pedal along the wide dirt road through a series of climbs and descents. The worst climbs are all behind, so enjoy yourself.

At mile 8.3, you will come to a large culvert with a clear stream running through it. An old cabin sits beside the stream. This is a good place, if you are so inclined, to fill up water bottles and cool off. (Be wary of drinking from small mountain

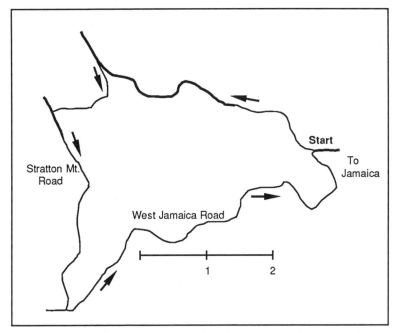

brooks — with more and more development in the watersheds, the possibility of contamination has increased.)

Cruise along for another half mile and just after you pass the Stratton town highway garage, you will intersect with the West Jamaica Road at mile 8.9. What follows may very will be the easiest and most enjoyable six miles you will ever ride. Take a left and follow the brook back to the starting point, ignoring all side roads, enjoying the sandy road. This will be comfortable downhill riding without any steep sections to worry about. You will pass many camps and home as you spin along. At mile 10.4, you'll pass the Forester Pond intersection but just bear right, following the brook. This is a fitting end to a ride that made you huff up some hills. When you get back to the car, why not try a wade/swim in the Ball Mountain Brook. See if all the snow on Stratton has melted yet.

Pleasant Valley Loop (11.5 Miles   Class 3)

Short Summary

A hill-climber's special. This is a short loop which features two long climbs and a rolling descent back to the start. For conditioned riders who want a quick challenging ride.

Directions To Start

Take Route 30 north from Brattleboro for 5.5 miles. Look for a green road sign on the left for "Stickney Brook Road." If you come to a narrow steel bridge on your right across the West River, you have gone too far. There is parking on the west side of Route 30 at the starting point.

Full Description

Before you start this challenging ride, you might want to warm up by riding on the shoulder of Route 30 for a few minutes. Take a moment to look at the pretty brook which rolls over a series of flat rocks. Stickney Brook is a favorite trout stream for local anglers.

The ride starts with a climb. Start up Stickney Brook Road, climbing and continuing straight where the "Road Narrows" sign appears. (You will be returning via the road that angles off to the right.) After just .2 miles, you'll be faced with a "V" in the road — of course, you want the left fork, the one that seems to go straight up. Get into a granny gear and climb sharply for a half mile. This is one of the toughest uphills in this book and you're tackling it right away. As some attractive farm fields show up on your left, the worst is over. You'll pass a small farm and at mile 1, the climb lessens to a gentle series of ups and downs. A quarter mile later comes the first downhill and at mile 1.5, you will come to a triangle intersection. Take the right fork up the hill. (The left fork goes to Brattleboro.)

The area through which you are riding is within the watershed for the Town of Brattleboro so you will note many warning signs posted along the way. That's why there will be little development in the next section of the ride.

After a short climb, you will come to some outbuildings and an old one-room schoolhouse (circa 1833) that has been converted into an environmental education center for children of the area. At the intersection, turn left, ignoring the "Road Closed" sign. That's for motor vehicles in the winter.

This is Gulf Road, a narrow thoroughfare that is not maintained ("We run the grader over it once a year," says the Town Highway foreman), and it will provide some nice easy backcountry riding for the next half mile before starting down. The ride is now generally all downhill, with one steep drop, until you intersect with the Sunset Lake Road at mile 3. And guess what? You are about to regain the elevation you just lost, and then some. Turn right and watch for traffic — this road can be busy at times. Many residents commute to jobs in Brattleboro and the environs.

Get set for a two mile climb. First, you'll pedal on nice rolling terrain for the first .5 miles and then the uphill starts. Watch for horses on your right as you climb since you are approaching a farm/stable. At mile 5.5 the road finally levels and starts downhill — keep straight ahead. Enjoy some easy recovery riding — it is nearly all downhill from here to the start. At mile 6.4, start down and ignore any roads or paths branching off until you come to Ravine Road, a right turn at mile 6.8.

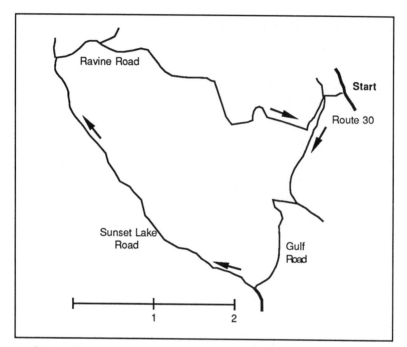

Coast down Ravine Road and after a half mile, bear right down the narrower Stickney Brook Road. (The left fork, Betterly Road, loops back but has more climbing on it.) Enjoy the narrow shady back road but expect several steep downhills and possible rough road conditions. At mile 8.5, the road makes a quick hairpin to the right across a small brook and then has two more sharp descents. As you approach Route 30, there will be more homes scattered along the way. At mile 11, the route intersects with Leonard Road. Take a right down the hill and soon you will come to the first intersection you encountered. Continue left down to the starting point.

Be sure to explore the brook before you leave — it is a lovely setting for the end of a good mountain bike workout ride.

Turkey Mountain Loop (18 Miles Class 3)

Short Summary

A steady but moderate climb at the start, a one mile stretch of "push your bike trail," and a spectacular picnic spot mark the first half of this ride. The second half consists of several long downhills, steady climbs and spectacular views to the west. A screaming 2.5 mile downhill provides an exciting finish. .

Directions To Start

Take Route 30 north from Brattleboro for 21.5 miles to West Townsend. The ride starts at the Country Store, next to the church. Park on the end of the lot near the hedges. The store supports cyclists by offering food, sports drinks, and an outside spigot to fill water bottles.

Full Description

Starting at the Country Store, head west for a gentle warmup on Route 30. You'll pedal past the highway garage and after 1.5 miles, pass the intersection with Route 100. As soon as you ride across the bridge spanning Turkey Mountain Brook, take a right turn onto the dirt road. Your legs should be nice and loose for the fun ahead.

The first mile and a half on Turkey Mountain Road affords some easy riding with gentle climbs. A sparkling brook on the right and a series of stone walls grace the road as you ascend. Watch for streams coming down off the flanks of the hills — some are nearly dry in summer but spectacular in the spring. A mix of year-round and vacation homes dot the road.

At mile 3.9, there will be a European-style log home called "Flower House" on the left. Pause and check out the small pool and large moss-covered boulder. After a short climb, you will have a level stretch with many granite outcroppings and a long bog lined with stark dead spruce trees. You might want to stop and notice how still it is up here. The road starts uphill again for a half mile of climbing from mile 4.5 to 5.0 and then you'll lose the elevation with a quick descent. Watch the loose gravel.

Just after another picturesque beaver pond on the right, the road pitches down steeply. Before you get going too fast, look to your right for an old stone foundation. What do you think it was, a cellar hole? A grist mill? Respect the "No Trespassing" signs posted here.

Turkey Mountain Road climbs for several tenths of a mile past what used to be a farm. Fields on both sides are overgrown with weeds. Note the line of ancient maples where sap buckets once hung and the wonderfully symmetrical stone wall. That mountain off to your left with the exposed granite flanks is Shatterack Mountain. At the end of the travelled road, you'll come to an A-frame but press on, the right-of-way goes to the east of the house, onward and upward.

Expert mountain bike riders will love the next section but the rest of us will do some pushing as we traverse the dirt bike/jeep trail. The path is very rocky in spots and is a steady climb for three-quarters of a mile. Take your time and ride when you can and push when you have to. As you come out into the clearing for the power line, pause for a moment on the conveniently-placed rock outcropping. Down below, you may hear the Hamilton Falls sawmill at work.

The last quarter-mile of the trail is downhill but again, is "expert level" riding at times. There are lots of stones and rough

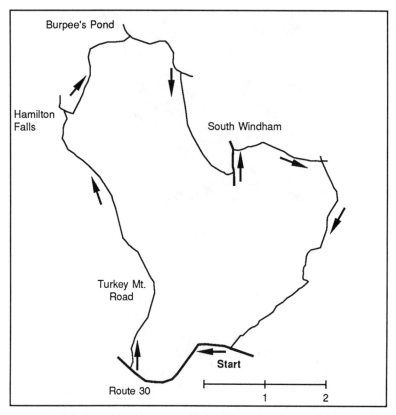

spots so if you ride it, stay off the front brake and keep your weight back. At mile 6.8 you will come out on to the dirt road. Take a left, roll by the sawmill, and just before starting down a steep hill, turn at the sign for Hamilton Falls. Walk you bike through the woods to the site — you a going to be pleased at how pretty it is, truly "the perfect picnic spot." (Mile 7.0)

Hamilton Falls is a torrent in the spring, dropping 125 feet in a white water cascade. In late summer, the brook slows to a trickle and several large pools of clear green water are revealed in the granite face. This unique geological formation is a dangerous spot — signs warn that nine people have lost there

A pool cut out of the granite at Hamilton Falls

lives here. Have a snack and admire the view but if you want to wade, do it well upstream.

After stopping at the falls, backtrack up the road by the sawmill. Stay on the main dirt road — you have some gentle farm country riding ahead. At mile 7.5 you will pass a deserted sugar house and a moment later, an abandoned sawmill. The road is lined with stone walls, hayfields, and a smattering of white birches. At 8.0 you will pass the Dutton's Holstein farm. Swing to the right at the next intersection, still on the main dirt road, and look off to the right. That's Turkey Mountain.

The next mile and a half has a couple of challenging climbs coupled with some easy riding followed by a great little downhill. As you approach the pine tree lined section, you've come to Burpee's Pond which is pretty in the spring but choked with lily pads in August. Look way north and you can see the white spire of the church in Windham peeking up through the trees. The intersection at the end of the pond is mile 10.

Turn right at the intersection, bike by the old dam and climb up the hill. Just before the top of the rise (Mile 10.4), turn right onto a narrow lane (unmarked at this end) called Olde Cheney Road. You have two miles of downhill ahead. The road looks like a driveway at times — narrow with grass growing in the middle — but keep going. Soon, off to your left, you'll spot the hamlet of South Windham. After a short climb, intersect the paved road at mile 12.3.

Turn left and head north on pavement for just a few hundred yards. Take the paved right turn that goes immediately to dirt. This is Chase Road (unmarked.) If you get to the church in South Windham, you've gone too far on pavement.

Now let's be honest — you're going to climb again on Chase Road but it is not that bad, you are already high above West Townsend. The views make this loop worth the extra energy.

Chase Road starts with an easy uphill and in the first 1.5 miles, has a series of tough little climbs. But that is it — no more climbing after mile 14. After the last steep ascent, you will come to an intersection. Bear right and get ready for a welcome downhill. You'll read "Don & Peggy's Orchard" on a building as you roll past and near the bottom of the hill.

The views during the next mile are excellent. That is the Stratton Mountain ski area off to the west. Relax and enjoy the high elevation riding, checking brakes for the descent ahead. What a drop it is! Steep and two and a half miles long, the road has one sharp "S" turn and washboard and loose gravel in spots. Take the bumps with your legs and keep speed under control. After one last steep drop, you'll have a right turn onto a paved street and be right back at the starting point on Route 30. Use caution crossing, your legs may be a little rubbery from that descent. Enjoy a soda at the store. You have earned it.

Weston Loops

Weston is a tourist mecca, located smack on Route 100 and graced with a classic Town green complete with bandstand. Centrally located, the Town is an hours' drive from Brattleboro, two hours from Albany, three from Boston. The Weston Playhouse, the oldest professional summer theater in the state, is one of the major attractions in the area. Perhaps you'll want to stay and catch a show. (Call 802-824-5288 for information).

Mountain bike rides in Weston are hilly with challenging climbs onto the surrounding ridges and exciting descents back to Town. All the attractions (country stores, bowl mill, fudge factory to name but a few) are waiting for you when you return. It is definitely a place to use as a base for some exciting rides.

Hapgood Pond (13 Miles   Class 2)

Short Summary
Hapgood Pond is a U.S. Forest Service recreational area that was built in the 1930s by the Civilian Conservation Corps. A favorite of locals and summer residents, it has a nice swimming beach as well as fine camping and picnic sites, so bring your bathing suit. The route has an initial steep climb and descent, but the rest is easy riding. You'll have to climb the same hill on the way back before the final downhill back into Weston.

The Weston Playhouse marks the start of the Weston loops

Directions To Start

The Village of Weston is located on Route 100 and is easily reached by a number of routes. From I-91 Exit 6, take Route 103 through Chester and look for the right turn to Weston. From Manchester, take Route 11 to Londonderry and then Route 100 five miles north. The village green has parking on the west side.

Full Description

Head west out of Weston, across the bridge by the Wilder Homestead Inn. Take the sharp left (Landgrove Road — unmarked) and climb/push up the steep hill. The pavement ends at .5 miles and you will continue climbing for another half mile. As you crest the hill, pause and look back at the lovely view.

Continue straight ahead down the hill, ignoring the left turn onto Holden Hill Road. For the next two miles, there's some rolling country riding to enjoy. Pass by Cody Road on the left

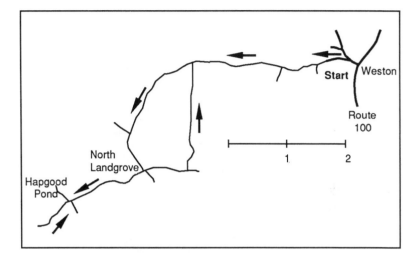

and at mile 3, continue past the road to the right. Coast down the
long descent and as you come to the Utley Brook intersection,
pedal straight ahead. This will be a pleasant level stretch with
meadows and a brook off to the right until you come to the
North Landgrove 4-way intersection. (Mile 4.6) Turn right on
the Landgrove Road and after two miles of easy riding, you'll
see the turn for Hapgood Pond. (If you'd rather bike than swim,
the National Forest Road goes ahead for a number of miles into
the Green Mountain range.)

Hapgood Pond is a great swimming site and has several foot
trails to explore. When you are ready to leave, backtrack to
North Landgrove and instead of taking the left at the Town Hall
(your previous route), go straight ahead for a mile of level dirt
road riding and take the second left, Cody Road, which is
unmarked, and which climbs very steeply. Once on top, you'll
pass a number of nice homes as you pedal to the intersection
with the Landgrove Road. Turn right, climb to the high point
overlooking Weston, and descend to your starting point.

Weston Priory Loop (13 Miles   Class 3)

Short Summary
Starting off easy, this ride offers a pleasant stop at the Weston Priory and then, after a few miles of easy going, a rugged climb into the National Forest and a long descent into Weston.

Directions To Start
The Village of Weston is located on Route 100 and is easily reached by a number of routes. From I-91 Exit 6, take Route 103 through Chester and look for the right turn to Weston. From Manchester, take Route 11 to Londonderry and then Route 100.

Full Description
Head west on the paved road which crosses the West River and immediately starts uphill by the Wilder Homestead Inn. Keep climbing on the paved road straight ahead. You will be on the Lawrence Hills Road which turns to dirt a half mile from the start of the ride. Follow the signs marked "Kinhaven."

After a quarter mile of level riding, you will start to climb, passing several lovely country homes with magnificent views. After a half mile, the road pitches down by the summer music school called Kinhaven. Located on an attractive old estate, Kinhaven has free concerts on Friday and Sunday afternoons.

Ahead, you will soon see a clearing and the roof of the Town Garage. At the intersection, take a right and then an immediate left on the unmarked dirt road. It is 1.5 miles, with several steep climbs, to the Weston Priory. The Priory, a monastery for

Benedictine monks, is set up to handle visitors and has a shop with such things as homemade cider and arts and crafts made by the monks. There is a public prayer service each day. It is a lovely piece of Vermont, well worth a stop.

To continue the ride, backtrack down the mile and a half you

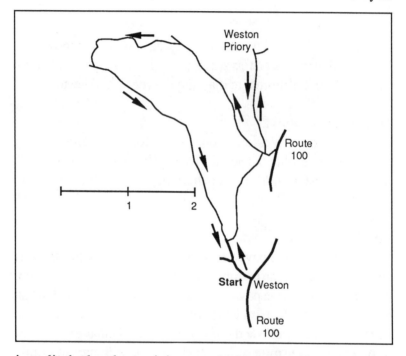

just climbed and turn right, past the highway garage, crossing the Greendale Brook at 5.5 miles. You will have some easy riding for about a mile with the brook on your right before starting a moderate climb through a forested area. At mile 7.0, you will come upon several homes and cross the bridge over Coolidge brook. Take the road marked "17" and get ready to climb. You will be climbing up the Coolidge Brook Road for a mile and a half on a narrow gravel road, passing the National Forest Boundary early in the ascent.

The climb is steep so take your time. This may be a good place to walk the bike for a while. Note the brook — it is very "flashy" and wreaks havoc in the spring — and has many fallen

The Weston Priory

trees and exposed boulders along the stream path. After a mile of uphill, there'll be a red cabin on the left. Continue up until you come to a left turn at mile 8.0. You are nearly at the top.

After the left turn, the route crosses the brook and then there is the last half mile climb and it is steep. Stop to notice how remote this part of the ride is and how quiet things are.

The road starts down in a series of descents and level spots, perfect for riding. Look ahead and catch the views of the mountains across the valley. After three miles of downhill, you will whip by Parker Lane on the right and arrive at a stop sign. This is the road you began the ride on. Take a right and you will soon be on pavement, coasting back to Weston. Perhaps it is time to get an ice cream cone, sit in the bandstand, and think about the neat mountain bike ride you just had.

Weston Short Loop (8.5 Miles   Class 3)

Short Summary

If your time is limited and you just want a taste of back road riding, here's a short loop with a couple of very steep climbs and descents. You will see some great views and ride down one of the steepest dirt roads in Southern Vermont. (You can add another seven miles of difficult riding if you are looking for more of a challenge.)

Directions To Start

The Village of Weston is located on Route 100 and is easily reached by a number of routes. From I-91 Exit 6, take Route 103 through Chester and look for the right turn to Weston. From Manchester, take Route 11 to Londonderry and then Route 100 five miles north. The village green has parking on the west side.

Full Description

You may want to warm up with a sightseeing ride around Weston Village for this route begins with a difficult climb. Head west out of Weston, across the bridge by the Wilder Homestead Inn. You will climb past the aptly named Church On The Hill which was built in 1838 and now serves as the Weston Community Church. Instead of proceeding ahead as in the Weston Priory ride, take the sharp left (Landgrove Road — unmarked) and climb/push up the hill. The pavement ends at .5 miles and you continue climbing for another half mile, ignoring the left turn at mile .6. As you crest the hill, pause and look back at the lovely view. What a tough start to a ride!

Continue ahead on the easy downhill, being ready for a left turn onto Holden Hill Road in a quarter mile. Keep your speed up in the turn and as you descend because there is a steep climb ahead. When you get to the top (1.6), check out the mountains off to the east. You are coming to the Holden Hill Farm whose Holsteins must have one of the prettiest views in Vermont. Keep an eye open for farm dogs. (We encountered none).

As you traverse the ridge, you will go by a number of camps and homes and enjoy a series of glides and climbs — this is mountain biking at its best. Better yet, you are about to get some nice downhill riding.

There's a steep downhill at mile 2.5 with a left turn at the bottom. After a half mile of descent, it levels off, so go ahead and enjoy some of the momentum you have built up as you coast down the maple-lined road. At 3.7 miles, you will come to a four-way intersection, all unmarked. Press on straight ahead ignoring the roads off to the left and as you ride downhill, and prepare for a steep downhill — repeat, steep downhill. (Check your brakes, get your weight back, use your rear brake.) This very steep descent has loose gravel and washboard conditions but it is over quickly. You'll pass a small cluster of trailers and homes, and a bright red barn will greet you as you roll out to the pavement at Route 100. (If you need to cut things short, you can follow Route 100 north to Weston — it is 2.5 miles on paved roads.)

To continue, turn left on Route 100 for a short stretch, crossing the West River and then, at mile 4.8, turn right on the paved road. (Stage Coach Road - unmarked) The road turns to dirt immediately and you will come to a four way dirt intersection. Take the sharp left by the church (which is now a home), and pedal or push your bike up the steep hill. This is the cousin

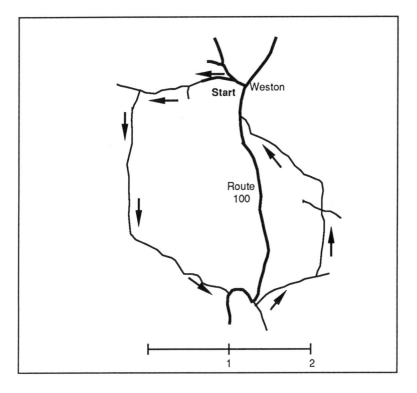

of the hill on the other side of Route 100 which you just came down. The climb gets easier at mile 5.4, and if you look off to the right, you can see the Magic Mountain ski slopes. After a short stretch of easier riding, you'll begin climbing again and soon come to an intersection.

Turn left on Piper Hill Road (unmarked). After a half mile of level riding, you will start a climb toward a four way dirt intersection at mile 6.6. Continue straight ahead and after a series of shallow climbs and descents with some nice views of the hills across the valley to the west, you'll have a half mile downhill back to Route 100. Turn right and you can see the starting point just up ahead.

PART 3

Resources

163

RESOURCES

Bike Shops

Bicycle shop personnel can not only adjust your derailleur, they can also steer you toward some off-road riding in their area. Some shops conduct mountain bike rides and races. Patronize them for equipment items such as bike bottles, sunglasses, topo maps — the things that make for a good ride. Most shops are open Saturday but many are closed Sunday in the summer so call ahead.

Battenkill Sports
RR #1, Box 610
Manchester Depot   (802) 362-2734

Brattleboro Bicycle Shop
178 Main St.
Brattleboro   (802) 254-8644

Mountain Bike Peddler
954 E. Main St.
Bennington   (802) 447-7968

Specialized Sports
Putney Road
Brattleboro   (802) 257-1017

The Mountain Goat
Route 7A, Box 2182
Manchester (802) 362-5159

Up & Downhill
160 Benmont Avenue
Bennington   (802) 442-8664

Vermont Pedal Pushers
Route 11/30
Manchester Center   05255

West Hill Shop
Putney   (802) 387-5718

Tour Organizations

Vermont has a number of bicycle tour groups which ply the roads of the state and have operated for over a decade in some cases. Many have developed mountain bike tours and more undoubtedly will as the sport continues to develop. If you are looking for professional guidance and support, one of these groups may be the ticket. There is a vast array of services available: you can rent bikes or bring your own, have professional trip planning and be led by experienced riders or you can do your own thing. The groups providing mountain bike tours in southern Vermont are marked "SV."

Bicycle Holidays (*SV)
RD3, Box 2394
Middlebury 05753
(802) 388-BIKE

Craftsbury Mt. Bike Center
Box 31
Craftsbury Common 05827
(802) 586-7767

Cyclery Plus
36 Route Four
West Woodstock 05091
(802) 457-3377

N.E Bicycle Tours (*SV)
Box 26
Randolph 05060
(802) 728-3261

Vermont Bicycle Touring
Box 711
Bristol 05443
(802) 453-4811

Vermont Country Cyclers
Box 145
Waterbury Center
(802) 244-5215

Vermont Mountain Bike Tours
Box 541
Pittsfield 05762
(802) 746-8580

Mountain Bike School

While mountain bikes are easy to ride, when one plans to try serious off-road riding it is important to learn the correct technique. Southern Vermont boasts its own mountain bike school, located at Mount Snow, where you can learn riding skills as well as bike maintenance and map reading, and combine it with a Vermont vacation.

The Mountain Bike School and Touring Center
Mount Snow Resort
Mount Snow 05356 (800) 451-4211 or (802) 464-3333

Books

Coello, Dennis   *The Complete Mountain Biker.*
Lyons & Burford, 1989.

Busha, Willam   *25 Mountain Bike Tours in Vermont.*
Backcountry Publications, 1989.

Kelly, Charles   *Richard's Mountain Bike Book.*
Ballantine, 1988.

Sloane, Eugene   *Complete Book of All-Terrain Bicycles.*
Simon & Schuster, 1985.

Van der Plas, Rob   *Mountain Bike Book: Choosing, Riding & Maintaining the Off-Road Bicycle.*   Bicycle Books, 1988.

Periodicals

Bicycling
Excellent articles on training, technique and equipment from Rodale Press. Covers both road and mountain biking.

Bicycle Guide
A nine times a year magazine from Boston with articles and a Fat Tracks section on mountain biking

Mountain Bike Action
An irreverent West Coast monthly with good racing and technical articles.

Mountain & City Biking
A glossy look at all aspects of all-terrain riding.

Guides

The Vermont Atlas and Gazetteer   *The Vermont Road Atlas and Guide*
DeLorme Mapping Company   Northern Cartographic
P.O. Box 298   P.O. Box 133
Freeport, ME 04032   Burlington, VT 05402

Topographic Maps

Available at bike shops or bookstores or from:

U.S. Geological Survey   U.S.D.A — Forest Service
Box 25286, MS 306   Box 1940
Federal Center   Manchester Center, VT 05255
Denver, CO 80225   (802) 362-2307

Organizations

National Off-Road Bicycle Association (NORBA) -- now USCF

International Mountain Bicycling Association (IMBA)
Route 2, Box 303
Bishop, CA 93514
(619) 387-2757

United States Cycling Federation (USCF)
1750 East Boulder
Colorado Springs, CO 80909
(719)`578-4581

Glossary

Beartrap Pedal — the pedals on most mountain bikes which are sized to provide more contact with the foot and have ridges to keep your shoe from sliding off.

Bottom Bracket — the workhorse section of the crank assembly consisting of a spindle, bearings, several bearing cups and adjustment rings. Expensive bikes have sealed bearing cups or cartridges to keep water and dirt out.

Braze-on — brackets and attachments built into a bike for attaching water bottle cages, derailleurs, and brakes.

Brazing — the process, similar to welding, that is used to join bike frame tubes together. Special torches and brass rods are used to keep from deforming the fragile tubing.

Bunny Hop — a maneuver to jump over obstacles.

Cantilever brake — most mountain bikes have this type as opposed to the weaker side-pull brake used on road bikes.

Chainring — part of the crank unit. Most mountain bikes have three with the smallest having 18 to 25 teeth, the middle ring from 28 to 42 teeth, and the outer ring 48 to 52 teeth.

Chrome-moly — a steel alloy, chromium molybdenum, that is favored by bicycle builders.

Clean — a term used to successfully ride a difficult trail, such as to "clean" a section in an observed trials competition.

Component — other than the frame, anything on a bike such as brakes, wheels, and derailleurs.

Crank — two crank arms and a bottom bracket form the crank. Attach some pedals and you're ready to roll.

Criterium — a mountain bike race on a short closed course.

Dab — when the foot or hand touches the ground in trials riding. The rider is assessed one point for each dab.

Dropout — the "notched" part of the bike frame which holds the wheel in place.

Endo — a mountain bike racing term for an "end-over-end" fall from a bike.

Frameset — the frame and the fork. If you are into $2,000 bikes, normally you will buy a frameset from a custom builder and purchase components to complete the bike.

Freewheel — the set of six or seven chain sprockets mounted on the rear wheel.

Front derailleur — the mechanism that moves the chain from one chain ring to another on the crank. Located near the bottom of the seat tube.

Gauge — the thickness or thinness of the bike frame tubing or of a wheel spoke. The larger the number, the thinner the gauge, for example, a 12-gauge spoke is thicker than a 15-gauge one.

Geometry — the seat tube and steering tube angles and dimensions that affect the maneuverability of a bike.

Granny gears — the larger sized gears on the freewheel cluster that allow the rider to spin easily while climbing.

Gruppo — a group of components made by one manufacturer, such as a Shimano gruppo. (Pronounced "group-o")

Indexed shifting — a shifting system found on most mountain bikes which produces a click as the shift lever is moved from one position to the next. An accurate, easy way to shift.

Knobby — an off-road tire with treads designed to provide traction in dirt and sand.

Quick release — a lever and cam arrangement that allows easy removal of wheels and easy adjustment of the seat height.

Rear derailleur — moves the chain from one gear to the other on the freewheel cluster on the rear wheel.

Seat Post — the tube to which the seat is connected. Keep this cleaned and greased.

Seat Tube — the tube that holds the seat post and continues down to the bottom bracket.

Schrader Valve — the tire valve, used for autos and recreational bicycles, that is used for most mountain bikes as well. Road bikes use a smaller Presta tube valve.

Shred — to ride a difficult section aggressively, to "shred the trail."

Single Track — a narrow trail that has room for only one bike at a time.

Sneaker — a mountain bike tire, also called a *knobby*.

Technical Riding — terrain such as narrow trails, rocky sections, loose sand or mud that requires skill in bike handling.

TIG — abbreviation for Tungsten Inert Gas welding which is often used to assemble lower-priced mountain bikes.

Trials — also called *Observed Trials*. An event where riders maneuver through obstacle courses. Points are assessed for dabs and falls with the lowest score winning.

Toe clips — units shaped out of plastic or metal with straps to keep the foot on the pedals.

Trick — a mountain bike term of praise used to describe unique or unusual components or design, such as "the geometry and paint job of her new bike is trick."

Washboard — a rippled road condition that is prevalent on hilly dirt roads.

Water Bar — a diagonal ditch cut about 30 degrees to the road to divert water and to slow erosion. The deep ones are called *tank traps*.

Index

Order Form

No. of
Copies   Title   Price

[   ]   *Vermont Mountain Biking* $10.95
The best back road and trail rides in Southern Vermont

[   ]   *Central New York Mountain Biking* $12.95
The 30 best back road and trail rides in upstate New York

[   ]   *Canoe Racing* $14.95
The Competitor's Guide to Marathon and Downriver Racing

[   ]   *Skating on Skis* $ 9.95
Easy-to-understand advice on cross country ski-skating

[   ]   *Runner's Guide to Cross Country Skiing* $10.95
How to use Nordic skiing to supplement a running program

We encourage you to buy Acorn books at a book store or
sports shop. If you order directly from Acorn by mail,
telephone, or fax, prepayment by check or credit card is
required. Please include the price of the book(s) plus postage
and handling charges ($2.50 for the first book, $1.00 for each
additional books) as well as sales tax for New York
addresses.

Telephone or Fax Orders   (607) 565-4486
Provide shipping information as well as Visa or
MasterCard number and expiration date.

Mail Orders   Acorn Publishing
                 1063 Talmadge Hill South
                 Waverly, NY 14892

Name _____

Address _____

City _____ State ____ Zip _____

Telephone (   ) _____--_____